DON'T STOP AT GREEN LIGHTS

DON'T STOP AT GREEN LIGHTS

DR. PETER A. WISH
with **LINDA M. BLAND**

Adams Media Corporation
Holbrook, Massachusetts

For my daughter, Carly,
For my mother, Bert Sipkin,
For my brother, Barry
For my late father, Sidney
And especially, for the smartest and most loving person I know,
My wife, LeslieBeth

Published by
Adams Media Corporation
260 Center Street, Holbrook, MA 02343

ISBN: 1-55850-761-2

Printed in the United States of America.

J I H G F E D C B A

Library of Congress Cataloging-in-Publication Data
Wish, Peter A.
Don't stop at green lights : take charge of your life and
start achieving your dreams / Peter A. Wish with Linda M. Bland.
p.   cm.
Includes bibliographical references and index.
ISBN 1-55850-761-2 (pbk.)
1. Women–Conduct of life. 2. Success. I. Bland, Linda M. II. Title.
BJ1610.W57   1998
158'.082–dc21   97-37868
CIP

The writer and publisher have made every effort to trace the ownership of all copyrighted material and to secure appropriate permissions. Thanks are due to the following for permission to use the material indicated:

The Velveteen Rabbit: Or How Toys Become Real by Margery Williams (Doubleday ©1926)
Women, Work and Incest: Braving the Soul by Dr. LeslieBeth Berger (Berger ©1997)
Beat Stress All Day by Perry Garfinkle (Men's Health Magazine/Rodale Press, Inc. ©1997)
The Pursuit of Happiness by David G. Myers (William Morrow and Company ©1992)

This book is available at quantity discounts for bulk purchases.
For information, call 1-800-872-5627 (in Massachusetts, 617-767-8100).

Visit our home page at http://www.adamsmedia.com

Contents

Preface

While waiting at a traffic light one day in my Florida neighborhood, I noticed that the car in front of me wasn't moving, even though the light had turned green. I wondered whether the driver was distracted and lost in thought, or perhaps worried about venturing across the busy intersection. I waited patiently for a bit, finally saying out loud to myself in frustration, "Don't stop at green lights!"

Together we sat, suspended in time and sharing the fate of immobility, until the light turned red and then green again. I finally did get home that day, but the incident remained in my mind.

When I began work on this book, it occurred to me that, like the driver at that light, many women make important choices at crucial points in their lives — and then hesitate because they lack self-assurance. They see only red lights — all the reasons why they shouldn't act — and they sit helplessly as the abundance and joy to be had in life pass them by. Saddest of all, some of them wait too long. They never catch up with their own destinies.

Don't Stop at Green Lights addresses the dilemma of today's women who are getting older, living alone, watching their children leave home, or sensing a void in their work or personal lives — and don't know what their next move is.

My mission in writing this book is to help these women turn their red lights to green — and seize the moment to go forward. Today, more than ever, the directions they can choose from are virtually unlimited. They can travel to places where earlier generations of women never dreamed of venturing. They can chart meanings for themselves instead of blindly obeying traditional dictates or the expectations of others.

And, at last, the freedoms hard-won by women have been re-defined to match their most heartfelt aspirations. Feminism is no longer a new voice seeking to be heard. The women's movement has acquired wisdom and balance. It is no longer necessary to be a super-woman who "has it all." Women, for the most part, have acknowledged and understood their differences from men — right down to their definitions of enjoyment, achievement, and power.

This progress has not come easily. Over the past twenty-seven years, I have counseled thousands of women who were struggling with the complexities of realizing their full potential. One disheartening aspect of this otherwise rewarding work has been watching women — especially those with outstanding ideas and capabilities — come to a full stop whenever they reached a green light. Inspired by their dilemmas, I collaborated with them to devise ways to break through this impasse.

Think of this book as a gift from all these individuals whose journey I shared. They are its source. As I watched them dust off their childhood fantasies and bring them into adult focus, I knew that many more women could benefit from their stories and triumphs.

This is not just another you-can-have-it-all lecture. Unlike many inspirational self-help books today, this one is not about women from privileged backgrounds who became wildly successful. These modern-day heroines come from all social and economic levels: They are your neighbors, your coworkers, and your friends. As you get to know Annie, Carol, Libby, Sook, Julia, and the others, you will see yourself in them — and learn how to discover their resourcefulness and drive in yourself.

Nor will I tell you, in this book, to ignore your loved ones and dependents who might not be willing to go along with what you want. I know you have commitments you want to fulfill, and responsibilities you have no intention of evading. The advice in this book embraces the important role you play in the lives of others. The chance to invent a vision, shape it and go after it, without letting down or leaving behind the people who matter most to you, is what this book is all about.

ANNIE

Annie is one of those remarkable women who seem to pack more living into one lifetime than most of us would think possible. I met her for the first time years ago, when she came to see me for help in getting over her divorce. Her husband had walked out on her to take up with his secretary, leaving Annie with three little children.

The next time we met was when she returned for counseling — after she and her second husband mutually decided to divorce. Devastated by this repeat failure, she now had five children from two different men. "Two child support payments to chase," is how Annie wryly described her situation.

Then came a big surprise. When Annie reached her early forties, she fell in love with a man ten years older. "He had to practically drag me kicking and screaming to the altar," she said. "I was determined not to marry again, ever." Tragically, ten years later, Annie's beloved third husband died, leaving her alone once more. This was when she came to see me for the third time.

By now all five children were grown, so there were no more child support payments. Annie's third husband had left her little money to live on. With only a high school education and no history of employment, Annie found herself in a tough financial bind. Scrambling for independence, she took a job as a receptionist at a hair salon. But Annie felt hopeless and disheartened, afraid to make yet another start.

It came as quite a shock to Annie when, only a few months later, she was able to buy her own restaurant franchise and began making money at the rate of $75,000 a year — with options to double her income down the road. In a very short time, she became financially comfortable and personally fulfilled. How did Annie do it? Her sudden transformation from barely scraping by to "very comfortable" is worth exploring.

ALL IN THE FAMILY

Annie grew up in what she described as a typical Italian family. All day long, her mother cooked and cleaned: "A day didn't go by that my mother wasn't scrubbing floors and toilets or cooking vats of pasta sauce."

Annie was the third of four children. She had two older brothers and a younger brother with Down's syndrome. "I was mother's little helper. She had me cooking and cleaning and baby-sitting." Annie's parents were fierce defenders of the Down's syndrome son, making sure none of the older brothers or neighborhood kids picked on him. "We were a close-knit, warm family. But we had old-fashioned restrictions. Daddy was a plumber and made my two older brothers go into plumbing. They had no choice — they were told, 'You're becoming plumbers. That's it.'" Her two older brothers were expected to develop their own solid businesses. Her mother was expected to live with and care for the son with Down's syndrome "forever." Annie was expected to graduate from high school, work as a secretary, marry, and have as many children as possible. If she married a man in the plumbing business, all the better.

Annie said, "I knew their expectations. I heard them every day of my life. So and so would make a good husband. So and so would not. Be careful. Choose wisely. My brothers were even worse. They watched over me like hawks. I felt like all my life I had millions of eyes watching me. It was good — it made me feel safe growing up. But it also stopped me from making my own mistakes and trying things by myself."

When Annie was nineteen she married — who else? — a man in the plumbing business. He immediately merged his business with the family's, and they became a large plumbing and plumbers' supply company. "I got pregnant on my honeymoon, which was a weird thing, considering I knew absolutely nothing about sex. So here I was, the Virgin Mary myself, about to become a mother. A child having a child."

Annie quickly bore three children in a row. "They were ten months apart. I was no sooner out of delivery than I was working on the next one." But Annie said she was happy. "I had a family, lovely children, all olive-skinned and beautiful, and a husband with a good business."

Then — as often happens in family businesses — shortly after Annie's father died, the two brothers and Annie's husband began feuding about the direction of the company. Annie's husband didn't want to expand as rapidly as the brothers did, but they outvoted him. Soon, the business grew faster than the demand for its services, and the company almost went bust. "That was the worst time in my life. Now my husband had no reason to stay with me; he wasn't indebted to my family at all. We had never really gotten along anyway."

Annie's husband started another plumbing-related business and "fell in love with his eighteen-year-old secretary. She was young, bubbly — not burdened with children or stretch marks. I discovered the two of them making out in the storage room. Real romantic: kissing amid the toilets." Annie's husband soon left her for this secretary, leaving Annie with the children. "He did send checks — eventually. So I guess I wasn't as bad off as others."

During her children's school years Annie remained at home. "I never really thought about working. A mother's job was at home. Period. That's what I'd been shown and taught. And there was enough child support, so I had no reason to think about getting a job. I never crossed that bridge."

THE MARRIAGE-GO-ROUND
A few years later Annie met Mitch. She was taking her ex-husband's clothes to the dry cleaner's when they struck up a conversation. ("Don't even ask why I was still my first husband's handmaiden — I figured, what's the big deal? He pays the bills.") "Mitch was single, came from a huge family, and loved my kids. And he was a successful salesman. I thought, wow." They married after a brief courtship and had two children. "He wasn't a bad husband, just not great. Always working."

Once more, Annie found herself in a position where she didn't have to work or think about a career. She now had five children and was busy. "Mitch was this social climber, so we spent our time going to country clubs and charity events. Half the time I don't think anyone cared what the charity was. All a big bunch of phonies."

The more devoted to his career Mitch became, the less of a husband and father he was. "I don't think he ever fooled around on me, but work and status were more important. I hated the life, all the phony parties and fake friendships. Finally, we both agreed to say good-bye."

Mitch continued to support his children financially, but he didn't want to pay for what he considered the first husband's obligations. "Soon I had two ex-husbands who each felt the other owed me more money. I spent so much time in court I swore I'd never get married again. Of course, with all these money problems, you'd think I'd start considering finding a career of my own. But no. In my mind, women worked at home. Besides, my kids were still in school."

Annie lived on the child support, with occasional assistance from her brothers. "I never starved, but I didn't live really well." When Annie was in her forties, she met the love of her life — literally by accident.

"Chris plowed into me at a stop sign. He was so apologetic, no excuses or lame explanations. And he kept coming by to see if I was hurt or if I needed anything until my car got fixed. He was the nicest man. He worked as a rep for a medical supply company. He was far from rich or even comfortable, but I liked him. And he loved my kids. They were grown, self-supporting, but they still came home from time to time. It was important that any man in my life love them too."

Then, suddenly, Annie's mother died. Care of the brother with Down's syndrome was now her responsibility. "My brothers wanted nothing to do with him. And putting him in a home was out of the question. He was very high-functioning, but people have this bad view of Down's syndrome. I was afraid this might scare Chris off, but Chris loved my younger brother."

After much tugging and pulling, Chris and Annie were married. "I was scared — really scared." The marriage was a happy one, lasting ten years. Then Chris died.

"I was devastated. I thought it was the end of the world. My kids were grown, I was alone, in my fifties, wrinkles and sags and all, little money, a childlike brother to care for, and absolutely no career or even a work history. I got so depressed. My friends said I should be happy that I had finally experienced love in my third marriage. But it really didn't help."

What Makes Annie Run?

By the time Annie came to see me for the third time, she was more dejected than I had ever seen her. She was working as a receptionist at the hair salon, just making ends meet. She had had a falling-out with her family over the support of their younger brother, and as a result they were not being as financially generous as before. She felt absolutely hopeless and helpless about her situation.

Feeling that "life was over," she saw herself as "old, unattractive, unproductive, and finished." And she was scared to death to leave her younger brother home alone. "But what was I supposed to do? I must have called him every hour on the hour. I felt too guilty to put him in a 'facility'; besides, I had heard bad things about them."

I encouraged Annie to begin exploring her dreams — no matter how unrealistic they seemed. As with many of the women I've coun-seled, I asked her not to censor her visions and fantasies. Annie was amazed at what was on her list.

"You'd think I'd want to get married, have another man in my life — but no. In a weird way, my friends were right: I was lucky; I had found love once. If it happened again, okay, good, but the one thing I hadn't tried was a career. I was shocked that that was on my mind."

After compiling her lists, Annie realized she indeed had dreams, unrealized visions, and thwarted potential. For the first time she started to feel *hopeful*. "I didn't know what I wanted. And sometimes that brought me down. But I knew there had to be something."

I helped Annie avoid getting stuck taking too long to "find herself." After all, she had never really listened to her own thoughts about a career. She didn't know she even had any ideas. We explored lots of career paths, writing down possibilities, realistic and unrealistic. We brainstormed for a couple of months, going over long lists of potentials each week. Annie grew impatient, but we concentrated on understanding her dreams, interests, and skills. Because Annie had never worked, except as a receptionist in the salon, I administered some standardized career tests to help her identify skills, aptitudes, and preferences. Annie's dreams were so deeply buried, she needed to spend extra time on this part of the process.

What slowly emerged was that Annie loved working with people, had good managerial and decision-making abilities, and — most important — loved cooking. "Of course! How stupid that I didn't see it. I'm Italian — old-school Italian. The kitchen was a haven for me." Annie decided she wanted to run a restaurant. "That was totally unrealistic at the time," Annie later said. "I knew nothing."

Then Annie worked out a plan to make her dream more realistic. Her first small step to her goal was to work as a waitress. "Start at the bottom — I knew I had to do that. For me, at least. Now I really felt *optimistic*. I had a plan. I felt in command."

In six months Annie went from working at a small breakfast place to working in a more elaborate restaurant. She was a standout there. Her employers recognized immediately that she was reliable, pleasant, and intelligent, with common sense — "things I took for granted! I didn't know how rare they were." Her employer even gave Annie's younger brother a job as a dishwasher — a job he loved and performed well.

Soon her boss approached her with a business proposition. His son-in-law was opening a restaurant that was part of a well-known franchise chain. Would she be interested in managing it? He promised that she could take her brother along as a dishwasher. "I jumped at the chance. I mean, I *knew* the business. I felt I really understood people, and I was seeing firsthand the mistakes that were being made. I figured I could learn what I needed to know on the job."

The son-in-law trained her, and soon Annie was managing a well-known chain restaurant. "It was hard. There were days I went in scared to death. I had to learn supply ordering, all the details of how the national company worked. At first I felt lucky — dumb luck, I called it. But once I realized that luck *and* my skills brought the whole thing off, I began giving myself more credit. Only then did I seem to really catch on. That was important — I had to see myself as others saw me.

"And to my surprise — at first — the other employees looked to me for guidance, support, and leadership. I was so used to thinking of myself as a little girl who followed orders. Once I saw myself differently, I felt a real sense of *competence*."

After a few months, the son-in-law told Annie he wanted to exercise his option to open another restaurant. He offered her the chance to buy the franchise she was already managing. As regional director he would take a percentage of the profits, but she would own the restaurant. If she did well, he would offer her more opportunities to branch out.

"I was shaking in my boots. He offered to help me get loans. He was so nice and had so much faith in me — more than I had in myself. You know, during those times I went back and forth, up and down with this self-confidence thing, but I kept the negative voices down to a dull roar."

Annie indeed got a small business loan and bought her own restaurant. "It's really hard work: long, long hours. But my franchise has the lowest turnover of employees in the region. I don't know — I guess I have a knack for creating an environment where people feel valued. I know what it's like to be overlooked and not given chances."

Today Annie is considering opening a second restaurant. She's proud of herself and her brother. There are times she can't quite believe how she turned her life around. She's going forward.

Dr. Peter A. Wish
August 5, 1997
Sarasota, Florida

Acknowledgements

I will always be grateful to my late father, Sidney Wish, who instilled in me the desire for learning.

I wish to also thank friends, especially B. P. Smith, who helped me clarify ideas; my agent and collaborator, Linda M. Bland, for her organizational help; and Anne L. Weaver, acquisitions editor, who was brave enough to accept my book proposal and lend her expertise through the entire project. Thanks also to Ed Walters, editor in chief, for his valuable feedback. And, of course, thanks to Bob Adams and the others at Adams Media Corporation who gave me the green light to proceed with the book.

Last and most importantly, I wish to thank my life partner, colleague, and best friend, my wife Dr. LeslieBeth Berger. Her invaluable assisstance and clinical insights helped crystallize ideas, and she also helped write and edit several of the case studies included in the book. Her love, patience, intelligence, and confidence in me helped make this book possible.

Stuck at the Light

Did you ever play the game "Red Light/Green Light" when you were a child? It was pretty simple, if you recall. Your success depended on your ability to respond quickly when someone else told you it was time to stop or go. All you had to do was pay attention and follow the rules.

When women reach adulthood, they are expected to exchange their childhood games for reality. Instead, for many women, it often seems as though someone else is still telling them when the lights are turning red or green. Perhaps it's a mother or father or teacher, or a husband or lover, or a boss or colleague. Maybe it's a child, or even the child's teacher.

Even though a woman knows she's in the driver's seat, someone else can still be telling her to stop, go, wait, or hurry up. And she listens, because she cares about all these people in her life. She pays attention, and she follows their rules.

Does this sound familiar?

Even when she's, perhaps near the midpoint of her life, she still can hear the voices in her head — those backseat drivers who depend on her to get them where they want to be. But maybe she's beginning to wonder: *What about me? Is this really where I want to be? How did I get here, anyway?*

By now, perhaps, she expected to have been promoted at work, written a novel, traveled to China, or banked a million dollars. Instead, she's worrying about getting older, not having enough money for a comfortable retirement, growing old alone, or getting sick with no one around to care for her. She's anxious that life may be passing her by, leaving little time to accomplish her dreams.

A friend, acquaintance, or relative has recently died. Work is boring and stagnant. Worse, she's confused about what she wants to happen next, and nobody close to her seems to understand. Unfulfilled and disillusioned, she seesaws between rage and the blues, between the everydayness of her life and the lure of some untasted adventure.

She wonders what could be wrong with her, why these feelings are happening now. Why should she feel these cravings to risk it all, to flirt with change, to seek a second chance? Perhaps she daydreams about taking risks with sex, investigating an unpursued or lost love. Maybe she's thinking of a switch in careers, and for the first time she realizes that she's getting older. She wonders if it's just too late to start over.

I see so many women in this position, poised at some important intersection that can change the course of their lives. And yet they just can't seem to move forward. The light is green for them, but they can't see it. Instead, they listen to all the voices in their lives that urge them to stay right where they are: *You're too old. It's too late. What about us? You couldn't possibly.*

And what they feel, while they're idling at that light, is total desperation. Sooner or later, it's a feeling that culminates in despair — a hopelessness that can paralyze them for the rest of their lives.

You don't have to let this happen to you. This book can show you the way to achieve a hopefulness and resolve that will put your life back in gear. This method has helped many women learn to recognize the important green lights they face in the middle of their lives, and to move forward in whatever direction their dreams want to go. You'll meet some of these women in the course of this book, and you'll be able to judge whether their experiences are similar to yours.

If what we've been discussing strikes a chord within you, consider the possibility that you have stumbled into a highly important phase that many people encounter — typically between their mid-thirties and early fifties. You may find yourself reassessing your worth and contemplating the rewards that have resulted from your efforts so far. You may be suffering from unresolved grief over lost opportunities, and you may express this loss through voracious new appetites — but only after long periods of stewing. You can't have what you really want, and this makes you angry.

So you may find yourself resorting to dramatic acts that are inappropriate or damaging — and won't, in the end, really satisfy your craving.

Wait: It gets worse. On top of having all these unmet needs and longings, you feel guilty for having them, don't you? You don't think you have any right to be so hopeless. After all, lots of people would love to have your life. So you add guilt to the rage and the blues, and you transform that dissatisfaction with your life into disgust with yourself.

You may think I'm just talking about your run-of-the-mill "midlife crisis," and that this, too, shall pass. It's true that we all come to the stage of life where we must acknowledge that we're not going to live forever. But for women, this universal time of self-assessment has other features. This may be the very first time you've had a chance to think seriously about your life and what to do with the rest of it — to fulfill your own expectations and not someone else's. Trust this process: This is what a green light looks like. It's an invitation to take control of your own journey.

IT'S DIFFERENT FOR WOMEN

It's not surprising that you may have trouble seeing this problem as an opportunity. Since the beginning of time, women have been formally taught and programmed to live for and do for others. Female children were not generally encouraged to speculate about their futures, because their roles as caretakers were predetermined. Nurturing, not achieving, was the only route open to them.

Little boys, on the other hand, have always been encouraged to consider and role-play many different future callings. The bigger their dream, the more praise they received. Males were acculturated to construct original visions for themselves, and to revise those visions as they moved along. They were not cautioned to stop and listen to the voices of others, telling them when to stop and go.

But, wait, you say — that's not true anymore. This may have been your mother's reality, but it isn't yours. Baby boomer women (those born between 1946 and 1964) have many more options. They watch other women engaging in unique, gratifying activities and embarking on explorations their mothers never dreamed of.

It's true that the world is wider for you. In addition to the nurturing route that was always traditionally carved out for women, the achieving route has been opened for you, and you are free to travel that route. You can even pursue both routes at the same time — or first one, and then the other.

But doesn't this compound your anxiety? With more options open to you, and more demands on your talents, and more women making enormous strides that you may be driven to emulate or envy, don't you sometimes feel even more confused and inadequate? If you do, it's not surprising. You are in the transitional generation, dealing with a set of conflicts and expectations that no women have ever faced before. And, no matter what you think, I can guarantee that you weren't handed the tools to deal with these challenges when you were growing up.

Look around, and you'll see that those women who appear to have their acts more together than yours are embarking on the very same search. When three hundred career women between the ages of thirty-five and forty-nine were surveyed about their aspirations, the results were revealing:

35 percent were contemplating a major career change

45 percent had seriously considered starting their own businesses

38 percent were thinking of going back to school

33 percent were considering changes in their personal lives

36 percent were thinking about getting pregnant

For these women, motherhood had little correlation with their dreams. Whether they already had children or not, they expressed their frustrations in similar ways — with a desire to start over. To find their green light and go for it.

First, though, they must learn to recognize a green light when they see one. That takes vision. And it's not the sort of vision you were born with. In this book, you will learn how to discover a vision of your own future and make it work for you. You've already seen how Annie, after many false starts, managed to focus on her dreams and put them into practice. You too will go through the necessary four steps that will teach you to see your green light and move forward into the life you truly want.

Here are the steps you will master in this book:

Visionalysis. Before you can go anywhere, you have to know where you are. This segment of the book will help you define what your desires really look like. Is your current route — nurturing or achieving — the one you want to keep traveling on? Annie was surprised to learn through this process that she was drawn more to a career — achieving — than to the close family life she'd always had.

Visioneering. Once you know where you are, you must envision a destination. In this part of the book you will design a concept of the life you are meant to lead, trying out options until you find the vehicle that's right for you. Annie discovered that the kitchen of a restaurant was her natural home — a vision that felt right to her from the moment she worked it out.

Visioncrafting. Here you will work out the details of your new route that will take you to your goal, a plan that will get you where want to go. You won't want to leave home without it, because a solidly crafted vision will help you stay the course when times get tough. Annie decided to learn the business from the ground up, starting as a waitress.

Visionavigating. In this final segment, you'll get yourself ready to put your pedal to the metal! We'll discuss some roadblocks you may encounter along the way, so you'll know how to keep steering with your vision firmly in sight. Once Annie had the opportunity to own a restaurant, she worked out a way to fit this challenge into her life, so that she was ready to master it.

Throughout this book, you'll find exercises that will help you hone your own vision and discover your unique capabilities for realizing it. It's a good idea to start with a notebook of your own, dedicated to this quest. When you come to an exercise, turn to a fresh page in your notebook. You'll be surprised to see how far your visionwork can take you in a very short time.

Nervous? Afraid? Of course you are! Achieving second adulthood isn't easy for anyone, but for women it's an even more complicated process. Often in my practice, I meet women who have terrific visions and the ability to act on them — but they waver in their course simply because the people who matter most to them don't believe in them. In this book, you will learn how to rediscover your dreams and reach

your goals — and convince the people you love to come along with
you on this most fascinating and rewarding ride of your life.

> *"The minute you settle for less than you
> deserve, you get even less than you settled
> for."*
>
> —MAUREEN DOWD,
> SYNDICATED COLUMNIST

part

VISIONALYSIS

1

Adjust
Your
Mirror

CAROL

Carol, forty-six, was the chief librarian at a major city library. She had worked hard all her life, paying for her schooling by waiting tables in an exclusive restaurant. She had always been enterprising and ambitious. "There was a war going on inside me — even when I was little. On one hand I wanted that happy TV-sitcom family. On the other hand, I learned from my mother that no one was going to help me — especially not a man. My mother cleaned houses and took in sewing while raising my two brothers and me. I think I met my father once, when he came to take my brothers to a baseball game. That was it, as far as fathering went."

Carol grew up in the inner city surrounded by other African-American families; most other moms were single heads of households like her own mother. "I resolved that that was never going to happen to me. It was school and work first. Then maybe a man — if ever."

Much to her surprise, Carol did meet a man she liked and trusted. Shortly after graduating from college and beginning work, she married Darryl and had two children. She continued to work part-time, but when her husband left her for another woman, Carol resumed her full-time work at the library. "My sons were in high school; the one thing I had wanted more than anything for them was a stable home. And now I didn't have one.

"All my life I had watched Donna Reed and Doris Day on television. No black families were depicted on television back then; the sitcom families were my only frame of reference. At night I thought about this Donna Reed kind of family; I fantasized having that kind of life. And so what happens when I get it? My husband leaves.

"I guess all along, in the back of my mind, I had planned for this kind of thing. It wasn't luck that allowed me to get such a good job — I had educated myself and prepared myself for bad times. I knew I could make it on my own financially. I was a good mother, that's all I knew. But I hated that I didn't have what I envisioned as the ideal family situation. It broke my heart, it really did."

Bringing It All Back Home

Several years later, Carol remarried. By this time both her sons were in college. She married Gregory, a widower who was quite comfortable financially and had a college-age son of his own. He saw little need for Carol to work. "Besides," Carol said, "I was tired. As important as work had always been to me, I was tired. It was my turn to kick back and do something for *me*. And you know, I think I sort of knew then that something was missing from my life, but I didn't know what."

Before Carol could settle into a routine in her new marriage, her mother became ill. Carol approached her new husband about having her mother move in with them. At first he wasn't happy about sharing their new life with an ailing elderly woman. Finally, he said he would fix up the basement so her mother would be more comfortable.

About a week later, Gregory's son, who had been away at school, announced that he was transferring back to a nearby college and wanted to move home. He had learning and developmental disabilities and was finding full-time academics too hard. He needed tutoring, as well as some counseling to build confidence so that he could succeed. With their home now rather crowded, Carol's husband decided to build a new wing onto the house.

Suddenly Carol was living day to day with an aging and ill mother and a stepson who needed some supervision. "It was crazy. What with worrying about my mother, keeping her medication schedule, making sure my stepson received school help and guidance, doing everyone's laundry, and shuttling my mother around here and there, I was a wreck. Not to mention the noise as the construction crew tore down walls, whined away with an electric saw, and hammered into the evening."

"One night into my so-called new life, I woke up crying. I dreamed I was locked in a box with a hundred screaming babies — and yet, in my dream, I was smiling. I mean I was actually smiling. Exhausted, but smiling. Very strange. At any rate, the next morning, I said to my husband Gregory, 'I can't do this.'"

Perhaps you have felt like Carol at times. Caretaker overload can sneak up quite easily if you don't monitor it closely. And what you might expect to be a nurturing, dream-come-true experience can turn into a nightmare. Sometimes the *idea* is more appealing than actually *doing* it.

In fact, some women have told me that they welcomed home their adult children in the hope that now, since the children were more mature, they would have a better, more equal relationship with them. Young adulthood can be a trying time, and some parents who take in their grown offspring feel they are sparing them some of the unnecessary stresses they themselves had to endure.

Many have found, however, that living with a grown child is decidedly difficult — they come and go as they please, choose friends their parents don't like, and lead a life that often confounds the parents. Despite feelings of love and good will, often the arrangement doesn't seem to work as smoothly as anticipated.

Carol found herself in this kind of situation. "I had my hands and heart full — I knew I was tired, angry, yet somehow satisfied — and didn't know why or how. That's when I went for counseling."

Carol's most pressing problem was the loss of her dreamy expectation of a new and easier life. She had also lost her work-world identity, which focused on achieving rather than nurturing. And, most important, Carol had suffered a loss of a sense of competence.

"I loved my mother, and I couldn't do anything about her frailty. I loved my new stepson — he was such a great kid, really — but I couldn't help him much either. You have no idea how much I hurt seeing him struggle with his studies. I don't know why they promoted him in high school. Well, I just felt out of control. And I'm not the type to feel good unless I have control — lots of it. Looking back, I don't know how I made it through that rough period."

Learning to Hope

When Carol came to see me, she had begun to enter the *hopeless* stage. Feeling quite pessimistic about her future, she had begun constructing all-encompassing negative assumptions about her life: *This will never change. I'll never be happy. I've made a dreadful mistake. I'm too selfish.* Psychologist Dr. Albert Ellis calls this kind of negative, global thinking "awfulizing." Lots of people are pessimists, and many personalize their losses, believing they've been singled out for bad times. But women in particular are inclined to feel depressed, angry, and out of control if they see that their responsibilities to others are as great or greater than their responsibility to themselves. They often feel guilt-ridden, anxious, and frustrated when they perceive that these obligations to others exceed their ability to manage them.

As Carol sat in my office, dazed and immobilized by what she experienced as overwhelming stress, she still occasionally glowed in the midst of the darkness. In fact, she was deriving some pleasure from the unpleasant situation — she just didn't know why. Carol needed to understand herself and her needs better; at the same time, she needed to move to the *hopeful* stage.

We met several times and just talked about her family life, her expectations, her dashed hopes — and her fantasies. Through these explorations, Carol discovered she had a deep need for family.

"Don't get me wrong: My mother did the best she could — no, she did even better than she could — but I guess I always longed for that Donna Reed family. And I wanted to be like my mother — good and hardworking. But mostly good. My mother opened her heart and her house to everyone. I love her . . . . And, I would say, I respect her more than anyone on this earth. I guess I've believed all along that happiness is helping other people. We weren't really religious people, but we had Christianity without the church, in my house."

Here, Carol realized, was the source of her mysterious smile and the sense of happiness she couldn't yet explain to herself: All her life she had just longed to have a family. She "wanted to be a member of a family with a mother, a father, a child, and a sense of happiness," but felt embarrassed having such "common" desires. "I never had a father, I had a mother who worked all the time. I wanted the traditional American family. I guess I wanted the American white family — it's embarrassing to admit, but that's what I wished for."

Carol experienced this longing as what she called a "betrayal" of her black heritage. But I assured her that wanting feelings of safety, belonging, connection, care, and love are *human* emotions, not race-specific.

Carol worked hard on giving herself permission to want what she called "common" things. She eventually was able to enjoy this new family life she had created.

Carol was able to face her emotional roadblocks so she could move on to the *hopeful* stage. She learned to manage her anxiety about not working outside the home and to trust that her husband was not going to abandon her. After Carol reached some inner peace and acceptance about her needs, she was ready to tackle directly the daily problems that bothered her.

First I had her make a list of all the issues that really concerned her at the time. Then I instructed her to rank the aspects of her life that hassled her the most, in some kind of order. Doing this, Carol discovered that what bugged her most was the constant state of disarray in the house. Her mother would leave dishes and glasses everywhere; her stepson left his shoes and books and jackets in every room. What also bothered her was being asked to drive her mother somewhere on short notice or to leave the car available for her stepson.

Carol needed a plan. She began to delegate responsibility for daily household chores, and she established a weekly sign-up calendar so that she knew ahead of time her mother's and stepson's transportation needs. In addition, she recruited Gregory to help more around the house. Instead of constantly trying to fulfill everyone else's needs, Carol began addressing her own.

If you have attempted to get your family to give you greater cooperation at home, you may have encountered some resistance from them. Remember, if you start tampering with the status quo, your family may feel threatened, because mothers traditionally "do it all" in families — and people by nature don't like changing.

Eventually, Carol took greater charge of the situation. Instead of cooking meals one at a time, she cooked one large meal and placed portions in the freezer to be microwaved later if someone wasn't going to be home on time. She hired a part-time nurse to assist with her mother. Some glimmers of hope began to appear.

The small steps Carol took moved her from hopelessness and helplessness to hopefulness. Why? Because she reassessed her drive to be "good," giving herself a license to fulfill her own needs. She allowed herself to feel whatever she felt — without judgment. In a short time, her competent self began to reemerge.

Carol also needed to become more optimistic. She told me that what would make her feel better was to "get her husband to help more with his son's schoolwork." Of course, she realized that she had married a traditional, patriarchal man — in fact, that was one of the things Carol liked about Gregory. She just wanted him to be a little more flexible. She knew he would not naturally take on family chores, nor would he necessarily do tasks happily even when she delegated them.

After much inner focusing, Carol came up with an idea: her own version of "family time." The essential requirement was for each family member to be connected with the rest of the family; that is, to do something with at least one other family member each week — and not the same person each time. They could also fulfill the requirement by doing an activity with the whole family. Sometimes they watched movies together; sometimes Gregory helped his son study; sometimes the son helped Gregory with repairs; sometimes the son played cards with Carol's mother.

A funny thing began to happen: They learned more about each other, enjoyed each other more, and felt mutually respected, understood, and loved. At first Gregory fought it. But when he saw his son's work improving because he had invested the time, Gregory began to experience the satisfaction of connection. Carol now says, marveling, "I know this wouldn't work in every family. But it worked for us. We needed more togetherness. We weren't acting like a family."

Carol had a good point. There isn't any one antidote that will cure every family. You must find out what *your* family and situation can handle. The secret is in taking the steps to discover it. Gradually, Carol became more optimistic because she was able to construct a coherent and satisfying vision for herself and her family.

Over time, as Carol delegated and organized more family tasks, she gained power, authority, a sense of belonging, and a renewed sense of competency. Soon, other family members volunteered ideas. A year later, at Carol's final session, she told me: "Looking back, I wonder what all the fuss was about. The house is running smoothly. Mom is doing great and so is my stepson. Sure, I have a cleaning service twice a month, but basically, it's my home and I feel I belong there. I'm getting what I missed all my life. I know you can't redo the past exactly, but I have the feelings I always craved."

Six months later, I read in the newspaper that Carol was giving lectures to local service organizations about adult life changes and adjustments. Because we had worked so thoroughly on her vision, she understood why it was a success — understood so well that she could pass her knowledge on to others.

Carol's story demonstrates how very necessary it is to dig beneath the surface to perform a thorough Visionalysis. To learn the secret to happiness within her current swirl of misery and chaos, she needed to take a long, hard look at herself. She had to unearth and dust off a long-cherished childhood dream — her vision of a real, "common" family life — and locate the point where that dream and her realities could intersect. This was where she found her green light, in the notion that with her patched-together household consisting of a mother, a second husband, and a grown stepson, she could develop the solid bonds of togetherness under one roof that she'd always longed for.

This isn't your typical, storybook brand of happiness and fulfillment. It was a unique version that worked just for her. You can see why it was difficult for her to make this discovery. The evolution of Carol's family was not the obvious crowning achievement that society would expect from an educated and independent woman. But she was able to let go of such expectations when she saw how they were blocking her path. You can, too. In this part of the book, you will learn to perform your own Visionalysis, to get the clearest possible picture of your own personal path toward tomorrow.

American literature is rich with examples of the rewards to be found in this type of self-discovery. Hastening off on their journey to the Land of Oz, that magical place where they could find their inner powers, Dorothy and her friends were willing to brave any danger. What they could not see, distracted by all the trials they were forced to undergo, was that their inner powers had been with them all along. That's why it's so important to look inside yourself, deeply, *before* starting out. It's easy for others to advise you simply to "follow the yellow brick road." But what if it doesn't take you where you truly want to go?

Unlearning Helplessness

The first and most daunting obstacle that may be blocking your view of the future is something psychologist Dr. Martin E. P. Seligman calls "learned helplessness." Remember that old television game show *You Bet Your Life*, with Groucho Marx as the wisecracking host? Too many women believe they have already bet their life — and lost. They see their everyday existence as being out of their control. Their dreams traditionally get put on hold indefinitely, as they fantasize that some-day — just as on Groucho's show — they'll say the magic word and the little white duck will miraculously drop down to pay them off.

In the meantime, these women use helplessness to get what they want. Because of their deep need to hold onto attachments and con-nections, as Dr. Jean Baker Miller has explained, they fear power, see-ing it as a threat to their relationships. Women who exercise genuine power enable themselves, not others. Is it any wonder that, through history, women have been told that to be powerful is to be alone and unloved? Look at Greek and Roman mythology: The nymph Daphne, pursued by Apollo, could only remain free and strong by being trans-formed into a laurel tree. And Medea, the clever sorceress who helped Jason find the Golden Fleece, was abandoned by Jason when he no longer needed her powerful wisdom to help him survive.

Our modern mythology is full of stories about strong women who purposely avoid tragedy by weakening themselves for the sake of love. Rather than stand alone and unprotected, they fall into the arms of fate. They simply give up. Remember Scarlett O'Hara, who accepted the marriage proposal of Charles Hamilton because she realized that Ashley Wilkes had failed her? Fear of abandonment made her agree to marry a man she did not love; her genuine needs and desires were over-shadowed by a self-destructive drive to take whatever revenge she could against Ashley. Instead of drawing on her inner strength, she deployed her helplessness as if it were a sword — and she hurt herself badly.

Psychologists have discovered quite a bit about this giving-up response since Scarlett's day. They tell us — and this won't surprise you — that *learned helplessness* leads directly to *hopelessness*. Studies with animals demonstrate this connection. In experiments in which some animals were able to escape from an unpleasant situation while others were not, the animals unable to escape would eventually quit. They would give up and lie down helplessly, tolerating their predicament without resistance. On the other hand, when animals were taught that what they did made a difference, they developed control over their circumstances and learned to escape. By refusing to give up, they acquired what Seligman terms "learned optimism."

You know you have developed a case of learned helplessness when you find yourself trapped by tautological thinking — an argument that simply goes around in circles. Instead of adopting Descartes's bold proposition "I think; therefore I am," you may often find yourself accentuating the negative: "I think whatever I do won't help, so I won't do anything."

How can you break out of this hopelessness-helplessness cycle? Well, you can start by cheering up. I'm not kidding: Optimistic thinking is what counters pessimism, and pessimism is what fuels learned helplessness. Cognitive psychologists believe that learned helplessness is a disorder of thinking — that is, it can be treated and replaced with learned optimism.

One way to cure learned helplessness is by teaching yourself to take responsibility and even some risks. Changing what you say to yourself and how you say it is critical. This is an important component of your Visionalysis — breaking the cycle of hopelessness by dramatically shifting your perspective on your own situation. We'll start this process with a short exercise that I call the "Two-Minute Warning."

This is an imaging exercise that will help you place yourself in control — in the driver's seat, where you belong. Now is the time to regain your belief that you have a choice in almost everything — because you do! Sure, there may be unavoidable tasks, obligations, and limitations in your life, but you do have freedom — more than you may realize — to choose how you will tackle them.

For the moment, let's toss aside those constraints. Grasping the idea that you have more authority over your life choices takes a little imagination and some honesty regarding your own power. So have your notebook or journal ready. Let's get started:

EXERCISE 1: TWO-MINUTE WARNING

Pick a quiet time and place where you can concentrate freely. Now imagine that a bell rings and a little voice suddenly comes into your head and announces, *You have only two minutes to live.* Quickly — in two minutes or less!— write down the answers to these questions:

What would you do first?

What do you wish you had done in your life?

What do you regret about your life so far?

What would you say to people?

Whom would you like to be with?

Where would you want to be?

Although it's sort of scary to contemplate the end of your life, this can be an extremely constructive exercise. Suddenly, you need to prioritize what you value in life. Were there any surprises there for you?

The American politician and writer Clare Boothe Luce had enough careers, accomplishments, wealth, and adventure to satisfy several women. As she lay dying, she claimed that her life had been a failure because she never returned to what *she* considered her real calling: writing for the theater. This was her answer to the two-minute warning exercise. Don't let this kind of regret be yours.

Perhaps you began the two-minute warning exercise but got bogged down by all the reasons why you could never realize any of your desires. You may have thought the exercise silly or a waste of time because you believe, given your life situation, that nothing that you deeply desire can possibly come true for you. *What's the use?* you might say. *I'll never even come close to any of my two-minute warning goals.* This is learned helplessness, stubbornly blocking your path. We'll need to take a side road to get around it.

Don't make the mistake of seeing this tendency to give up as some character trait that you cannot change. Few people are born pessimists. Most negative thinking stems, reasonably enough, from bad experiences. No stage of life is immune from unhappiness, and the hurts of childhood often teach us to shrink from our own dreams.

But just as you gradually learned this helplessness — absorbed it as a lesson from all the events in your life so far — you can learn to do without it now. The stories you tell yourself about your experiences — your own interpretations and mythologies — are what determine their importance in your life. Often you are not aware of how you've internalized these bad events; how they've become a part of you. You may mysteriously feel as if these dangers are lurking, even now, just around the corner.

Think about what happens when you turn on a faulty old lamp and get an unpleasant shock. Every time you reach for the switch after that, you anticipate that you will be shocked again. Reflexively, you pull back as you approach the switch. This makes it harder to turn on the light each time.

We develop automatic defenses to shield ourselves from perceived harm, and fear is one of our most frequently used protective devices. Fear comes in many disguises: indifference, procrastination, laziness, worry, doubt, overcaution, or unwillingness to take a risk. Any of these automatic defenses can, over time, harden into the habit of learned helplessness.

As we move through Visionalysis, you will learn how to exchange your helplessness for hopefulness. But first, let's get an accurate assessment of where you stand today. The balance between your hopes and your fears is something that can be measured on what I call "The Mid-life Meter."

EXERCISE 2: THE MID-LIFE METER
In this exercise, you'll be asked to put a number on your responses to fifteen statements, according to a scale that runs from zero to 10. To see how this will work, try finding a number on the scale that accurately reflects your feeling about the following statement:

Life would be so much better if only I could be rich and famous.

Here are your choices:

0-Never feel this way

1-Almost never feel this way

2-Rarely feel this way

3-Only occasionally feel this way

4-Sometimes feel this way

5-Feel this way about half the time

6-Feel this way more than half the time

7-Feel this way often

8-Feel this way very often

9-Feel this way constantly

10-Am obsessed by this feeling

You can see how this exercise works. If you answered 3, this question is a passing thought in your daily mid-life. You're hardly in crisis. If you answered 8 or 9, it's something to think about.

Now, in your notebook, rate your responses to the next fifteen statements on a scale of zero to 10. Then total your score to find out how you rate on the mid-life meter.

Birthdays are something to dread.

I think about what I could have done differently in my life.

I feel trapped by my mortgage, my kids, my partner, my job.

Even though I'm in good health, I think about death a lot lately.

Younger people are more appealing to me and seem to have more fun than my crowd.

More and more of my time is spent away from family and friends because they are not stimulating or interesting anymore.

Sex with my partner seems drab. Wild and uninhibited sex appeals to me — especially if it's linked with a stranger or even a friend.

I feel that the best part of my life is over, that I have not lived it fully.

I'd like to be twenty-one again.

Things don't seem quite right in my life, but I can't figure out why.

I fantasize about a career or role different from the one I have.

I feel I have sacrificed my own needs and wants to satisfy my parents, my partner, my children, my friends.

My life seems out of control. Time is slipping away.

Activities and events I used to enjoy I now find boring.

I find myself making excuses for slipping out of work to walk, wander, window-shop, or just sit and think.

A romantic relationship outside my marriage has helped me feel better (or worse).

After totaling your score, locate that number on the ranges below:

0-45   You are fairly content with your life and its routine.

46-90   The higher you score in this range, the more ambivalent or confused you feel. You need to begin looking around at what's making you unhappy. You are an excellent candidate for exploring Visionalysis on your own.

✓91-135   You are often disillusioned or dissatisfied, and feel that you have no choice but to be unhappy. It's time to find out why — perhaps with professional help.

136-150   Crisis! People who score in this range may be depressed or headed for trouble without realizing it. Now is the time to take this book with you to a therapist.

So what if I'm unhappy? many women ask. *What difference does it make?* The pursuit of happiness isn't some self-centered indulgence for people with a lot of time on their hands. It's a matter of survival! It can mean the difference between life and death, for you and the people you love. Let's see why.

IT HELPS TO BE HAPPY

Studies of people who have lived through disasters such as airplane crashes and earthquakes show clearly that extroverts — those who think optimistically — have a higher rate of survival. It's not hard to see why: for these people, hope overrides their panic response. This allows them to go into a "control function," which enables them to take effective life-saving actions.

You may be interested to know that an actual physiological effect corresponds to an optimistic outlook. It takes place in the brain, where chemicals are released to trigger the control function. So your mental and physical survival is really very much dependent on whether or not you can form the habit of thinking optimistically. The crucial difference between forever stopping at green lights and managing to move forward bravely on a new road lies in your capacity to hope for the best.

> *"If you don't change directions, you may end up where you are going."*
>
> —LAO-TSE

By this point in your reading, you should have an accurate measure of your own state of emotion. You're probably realizing that you need to take some action to move from helplessness to hopefulness. This is a crucial element of Visionalysis, and the next chapter will help you isolate the fears that lie in the way of your progress. But first it may help you to hear the story of Deborah, a woman who thought she had nothing left to lose, yet managed to put aside her fears and assume the optimistic outlook she needed to survive.

DEBORAH

Twelve years into marriage, Deborah felt that her relationship with her husband was maturing nicely. Richard was on a tenure track at the university where he taught. Their three children were starting the school year with the confidence and readiness that she had worked hard to develop. She and Richard had weathered some adversity, and learned to support each other through these times. Their relationship was a romantic one, replete with flowers and loving greeting cards.

Back when their first child was born, they had made the decision that Deborah would teach music only a few hours a week, so that she could focus on nurturing the children in their formative years. Before her marriage, though she had an excellent undergraduate education in music, Deborah had been unable to find employment in her field. She had worked for a couple of years in a low-paying secretarial position before meeting Richard.

One day, to Deborah's utter horror, Richard announced that he was filing for divorce. He said he had fallen in love with a younger woman whom he'd met at an academic conference. Deborah was crushed. She became so depressed that she could hardly get out of bed in the morning to tend to the children. Her family came to the house for a few weeks to pitch in so that everyday chores would get done and the children would be taken care of. For several weeks, Deborah remained numb.

Then she began to give in to her emotions. In a fit of anger she rifled through Richard's bureau, looking for clues about their breakup. To her dismay, she found love letters from three other women in his past — one dating back to their first year of marriage. This only served to stun her more deeply with shame and fury.

Deborah felt both hopeless and helpless. Within seconds, her identity as a wife had evaporated. And she had nothing to replace it with: After years of nurturing and with no record of achievement in the outside world, her future looked grim. When the shock began to wear off, Deborah told me she couldn't believe she had been so badly duped: "I loved him so much and put my career needs on hold so he could screw around. Unbelievable."

But because we used her desperate circumstances as a starting point, Deborah's depression began to lift. Slowly but surely, we picked up all the pieces that were Deborah and put them back together again. Like Humpty Dumpty, Deborah had had a great fall — but she was able to acknowledge that she hadn't spent all her years just sitting on a wall. As she took inventory, she found three terrific kids who adored her and a family-of-origin safety net dedicated to helping her through. She saw that she had reasons to give optimism a try.

Actually making the shift from the low gear of despair to the high gear of hopefulness was harder, but we managed it with the help of her lifelong friend — music. I told her to play upbeat music whenever she was at home. I suggested that whenever she listened to music, she should envision herself playing it, teaching it, even composing it.

Finally, Deborah became optimistic. Instead of blaming herself for Richard's cheating, or submitting to the temptation of living the rest of her life saddled with regret, Deborah fought back. She discovered inner resources that might well have gone untapped had her life continued solely on the nurturing route.

Today, Deborah is not only back on her feet, but marching forward to her own internal music. Her three children have formed a thriving team, helping their mother and each other. Her divorce is not final yet, because Richard is disputing almost every term of the settlement decreed by the court, including child support. But Deborah tells me that discovering his unfaithfulness was the lowest point for her, so the dreadful details of separating their lives pale in comparison. Richard has already hurt her as much as he can. She now finds his previous and current behavior juvenile, even laughable.

If anyone had the opportunity to fall back on learned helplessness, Deborah did. She could have seen their breakup as an excuse to give up — to resign herself to her fate as a woman scorned, with her best years behind her.

But instead of letting that low point defeat her, Deborah used it as a springboard to greater heights than she would have achieved had this traumatic event never happened. Once Deborah let go of her illusion that her husband and marriage were her only future, she was able to shed her timidity in pursuing her buried passion: music.

Deborah no longer spends all of her energy seeking another person to care for her. She has realized she *was* a wife and is *still* a mother, daughter, aunt, neighbor — and perhaps best of all, musician. Now she is employed full-time as the music director for an entire school district. And she plays the cello professionally at synagogues, churches, and concerts throughout her city. Deborah is well on her way to physical, financial, and spiritual well-being. For her, the most dire challenge lay in regaining her hope. To do this, she adjusted her mirror to reflect the positive aspects of life without her husband. Armed with a Visionalysis that showed her the strengths to be drawn from a loving and supportive family, she found her direction at last.

At this point, what does *your* mirror reveal? If you're not yet mobilized by the vision you find there, don't worry. You didn't reach this crossroads overnight, and you don't want to go forward until the view ahead of you is crystal clear. In the next chapter, we'll examine why you might have the feeling you're in a rut — and getting nowhere fast.

chapter 2

*S*top
*S*pinning Your
*W*heels

W hen you picked up this book, it may not have seemed all that obvious to you that you might be stalled at a green light. In fact, many women today are more likely to feel as if they're constantly running red lights — that their days are a blur of perpetual motion, an exhausting road race that is anything but stagnant. Before they begin the process of Visionalysis, they often report that their biggest problem is that they are constantly running behind. Eventually, they discover that there's a bigger problem: No matter how fast they think their engines are racing, they've come to a full stop. They're not moving. Visionalysis is the process of finding out why.

> *"Myself and fear were born twins."*
> —Thomas Hobbes

Envisioning the rest of your life careening off on a new and different course can be scary. Even after you've glimpsed the enormous value of change, you may feel reluctant to face its possible consequences. Though logic may tell you that no one can predict what the future holds, your heart may still pound with undefinable anxiety and fright. For now, the solution is for you to shed some light on those fears, distinguishing the ones that are reasonable — those you can address later — from the ones that are merely serving to hold you back.

EXERCISE 3: CHECKING UNDER THE HOOD
Try this self-test to determine your current outlook and help you identify your fears. Then you can decide how your outlook can actually be turned around, to help you meet your own needs.
Take out your notebook and draw a line down the middle of a fresh page. In the left column list all your *Needs:* for example, connection to others in a work setting, financial security, respect from others, self-confidence, a meaningful relationship, educational progress, spiritual connection, good health, a sense of accomplishment, an ability to communicate, a stable home life, a comfortable home, freedom to do what you want, freedom to express your creative aspirations, travel, friendship, control, intimacy, sexual expression, feeling of being loved, support from your mate in your pursuits. Remember, these aren't just luxuries that you feel might be nice to have in your life; these are the requirements you absolutely can't do without.
Then label the right-hand column *Fears.* Think long and hard while listing all the things you fear: losing your identity, perhaps, or failing, being overwhelmed by new responsibilities, discovering that your relationships are not what you thought, breaking old patterns set by your parents, not knowing how to perform, being unable to control the outcome of your actions.
In my practice I've identified some common fears women experience as they pursue change in their lives. Feel free to add yours to this list, if they apply:

Fear of Not Being Loved.   Most people have the irrational belief that they should be loved by everybody. And they live in constant fear that they won't be.

Fear of Being Alone.   We are born alone and we die alone. But the fear of living alone can paralyze us. Although a certain amount of dependency is healthy, a desire for constant togetherness can stem from insecurity.

Fear of the Unknown.   People miss a lot in life because of this fear. True, there are no guarantees that new experiences will not sometimes hold danger. But individuals in the grip of this fear give themselves no opportunity to find out. As a result, the unknown becomes a larger and more frightening place to them the longer they resist it.

Fear of Aging. For many women, this is attached closely to appearance. Thanks to America's obsession with youth and prejudice against age, this fear can seem overpowering. Women who agonize about aging say to themselves: *I'm less important; I won't be attractive to men; I won't have status; I have diminished mental and physical abilities; I should get out of the way for younger people.*

Fear of Abandonment. This bottom-line fear for all human beings gets acted out in one of two ways: Either you cling so tightly that others can't possibly leave you, or you carry around a ten-foot pole, keeping others always at a distance. Either way, you create exactly what you fear.

Once you've finished your lists of needs and fears, read them over. It should be understood that some fears can actually help you. They don't necessarily have to work against you. For example, a fear of failing may motivate you to learn and perform better. A need to be loved may, in turn, make you a more lovable and loving person. Put a plus sign next to any needs and fears you can identify as potential strengths.

Next, place a minus sign beside those items that merely block your efforts. Fear of being alone, for example, could be a thoroughly negative trait if you were in a destructive or violent relationship. And if you are wondering how a need can interfere with your efforts, consider this: Your needs may not always be in your best interest, especially if they are unattainable. For example, if you are convinced that financial security comes with earning $100,000 a year, you may be setting yourself up for a big disappointment.

Now, on a scale from zero to 10 — zero being not that strong an asset or strength, 10 being especially valuable — rate each need you put a plus next to and each fear you put a minus next to. You may notice something surprising — something I've frequently found when helping people do this exercise: paradoxically, your most compelling need is often what you most fear.

Now add up the ratings for each column and compare the totals. Do your fears outweigh your needs? If so, this may be why you are stopping at green lights, even though you need and want to proceed.

FEAR ITSELF

I don't mean to suggest that the fears holding you back are necessarily products of your skittish imagination — something you can put on a list and then wish away. Your circumstances at the moment might be so restrictive or bleak that anyone in your position would feel trapped or severely inhibited.

Let's say you feel oppressed by your partner, whose insecurity continually discourages or even undermines any exploration of your own desires. You find repeatedly that what you do or say to him has little impact on his responses. If your husband discourages or outright prevents you from meeting friends or attending a seminar, for example, or if he checks up on you at unpredictable times to be sure you are not cheating on him, you can soon develop a monumental case of learned helplessness. You may have started out as a perfectly healthy, capable individual, but eventually you surrender more and more personal power over your life. When you make a suggestion, it is never taken seriously; if you object, the overreaction that follows is not worth the price you have to pay.

In a situation like this, the fear of criticism robs you of your initiative, thwarts your imagination, steals your self-reliance, and strangles your individuality. Self-esteem spirals downward, decomposing into depression, self-betrayal, even self-hatred. When you fight but still submit to unfair circumstances, you're struggling to survive in a world that betrays your hopes, values, and potential. Continually anticipating disapproval and coercion, you abandon your enthusiasm, your dreams — your self.

But even in an extreme situation such as this, when your fears are valid and directly connected to your current life, all that we've learned so far about optimism still applies. Even when you can't control anything else, you can learn to change your response to danger, by believing that what you do allows you to escape from the trap of learned helplessness.

If hopefulness can help human beings survive life-threatening disasters like crashes and earthquakes, it can help you survive a controlling spouse or a failed career. By making a list of your fears, and acknowledging them as real, you have already taken the vital first step toward shifting your life into a positive gear. And you are likely to discover, as did Susan, a woman I counseled, that what you fear is also what you thought you needed.

SUSAN

When Susan arrived at my office one morning, she felt as if she were being smothered. "Suddenly I awoke in the middle of the night and had trouble catching my breath," she told me. As we talked during the next few weeks, I began to see the culprit in Susan's marriage that was causing her anxiety: her husband Sean's overprotectiveness and domineering behavior.

"He wants to know where I am twenty-four hours a day, seven days a week. He checks the mileage on my car, he beeps me randomly during the day, and I get the third degree when I'm late coming home. And he's always finding fault with what I do. Nothing is ever right — our meals, his shirts, the house, you name it. He's even got the kids making fun of me. I feel totally overwhelmed by him. I don't know where he ends and I begin."

I asked Susan what attracted her to Sean. She told me she felt taken care of because he was always so "in charge" and concerned with her well-being. What she didn't realize was that Sean's apparent comforting and take-charge attitude was really a smokescreen for his need to be in control. Susan was on a very short leash.

If you find it surprising that Susan had to struggle to understand that her needs and fears were one and the same, take a look at your own list again. This time, do you see needs and fears that are opposite sides of the same coin? Could your need to be loved be feeding your fear of abandonment? Is your fear of failure the same as your need for self-respect? Understanding these patterns is fundamental in your Visionalysis. Only when you see the relationship between your needs and fears will they cease to be obstacles and allow you to transform them into the energy that fuels your quest.

As you're sorting through your fears, dividing those that are real — derived from the actual circumstances of your life — from those that are not, you will find that some of your realistic fears may have taken on too much importance in your life. They're valid, all right, but your habit of learned helplessness may have allowed you to overstate them. Consider whether some of the paralyzing fears unearthed through your Visionalysis can be downgraded to bothersome worries. Worries are a necessary part of life — everyone has them — and in a later part of this book, I will show you how to minimize your worries, making for a less bumpy ride.

For now, though, let's concentrate on defusing those fears that don't have to lie along your route. You've picked them up, somehow, in your travels through childhood and early adulthood. Now, your Visionalysis requires that you examine and discard the ones that are merely so much extra baggage.

If it's difficult for you to see the pattern created by your needs and fears, it could be that you're hiding them from yourself. Let's face it — no one enjoys confronting their deepest fears. One ingenious way to avoid such a close, personal reckoning with yourself is by letting your mind wander off to what I call the Land of If-Only. Instead of admitting that your own fears are blocking your path, you may choose to place the blame on circumstances beyond your control.

Let's find out if you've been escaping to the Land of If-Only.

EXERCISE 4: THE LAND OF IF-ONLY

Here are some hiding places people can frequent in the Land of If-Only. Be honest with yourself. Check off the ones you've been visiting lately:

IF ONLY I earned more money . . .

IF ONLY I had inherited money . . .

IF ONLY I could save some money . . .

IF ONLY I had the talent . . .

IF ONLY I had more education . . .

IF ONLY I knew how to . . .

IF ONLY I could get a job . . .

IF ONLY I could change jobs . . .

IF ONLY my employer appreciated my work . . .

IF ONLY others understood me better . . .

IF ONLY I didn't have to worry about what "they" would say . . .

IF ONLY I could get in with the "right" people . . .

IF ONLY I did not . . .

IF ONLY I had a business of my own . . .

IF ONLY I didn't have health problems . . .

IF ONLY I had more spare time . . .

IF ONLY I dared . . .

IF ONLY I lived somewhere else . . .

IF ONLY I had someone to help me . . .

IF ONLY I could get started . . .

IF ONLY I were free to . . .

IF ONLY I were younger . . .

IF ONLY I were not so overweight . . .

IF ONLY I had a better personality . . .

IF ONLY my luck would change . . .

IF ONLY I could live my life over . . .

IF ONLY I had had a chance . . .

IF ONLY I could get a "break" . . .

IF ONLY I hadn't failed . . .

IF ONLY I had made a different decision when . . .

IF ONLY others would listen to me . . .

IF ONLY I didn't have a partner . . .

IF ONLY I didn't have a family . . .

IF ONLY others didn't oppose my ideas . . .

IF ONLY I could marry the right person . . .

Now, for all the IF-ONLYS that apply to you, compose your own endings in your notebook. Write down any more IF-ONLYS that come to mind. When you are done, carefully and thoroughly rip up the pages you wrote them on. Tear them out of your notebook, and out of your heart and mind forever.

Why? Because the Land of If-Only is nothing but a dead end on the road to nowhere. It's the place where your hopes go to take a permanent vacation. If you let yourself travel too far down the route of pinning your dreams on whatever you can't have, you can forget about making it through the green light that's waiting right in front of your eyes.

Prince Charming and Other Fairy Tales

Let's return to that last IF-ONLY for a moment — the one about marrying the right person. This is a deeply instilled female fantasy. If you truly want to be the heroine of your own story, you must reject the illusion that some knight in shining armor will rescue you.

Today, companionship is not guaranteed: 43 percent of first marriages in the United States end in divorce, and 54 percent of subsequent ones do. Single, well-educated women over forty have a significantly reduced chance of marrying or remarrying. A quarter of the adults in this country live alone, and more than 63 percent of these single Americans are women. Among single adults over age forty-five, three-quarters are female.

Until you dismiss the outdated notion that someone else will totally protect and completely provide for you, you cannot become as personally effective and balanced in your relationships and in your life as you can be. So now it's time to lighten your load and rid yourself of all your IF-ONLYs. You'll be amazed at how much more powerful you will feel without them.

You've probably realized by now that these burdensome IF-ONLYs are a product of learned helplessness. So are their close cousins — unreasonable beliefs. These are none other than your own familiar fears in another brilliant disguise. Unreasonable beliefs come from clinging to fears that you don't need by restating them as part of your personal philosophy. The sooner you identify and modify your unreasonable beliefs to fit reality, the sooner they will stop coming between you and your dreams.

Read this list of common yet irrational beliefs, and see if they sound all too familiar:

When change occurs or I try something new, apprehension and anxiety are my only possible responses.

A perfect love and relationship for me are out there somewhere.

My value as a person depends on how others judge me.

My contribution to the world depends on how hard I work and how much I achieve.

When others disapprove of my actions, I've made a mistake.

I'm not very self-confident or assertive.

If I feel something strongly, then it's right.

Other unreasonable generalizations insidiously dictate our thoughts and actions: I MUST spend more time . . . . I OUGHT to be a better (wife, mother, daughter, mentor) . . . . I HAVE TO read more, work out more . . . and on and on. Many of these beliefs have been your faithful companions for decades. You adopted them to comfort and protect you, and to earn the approval of parents or peers.

"SHOULD HAPPENS"

Many unreasonable beliefs are easy to spot because of the one word they have in common: SHOULD. The most universal "should" in our culture is "I should be thin." If you have been "shoulding" yourself, now is the time to stop.

Shoulding is one way people strive for perfection. It was the famous psychoanalyst Karen Horney who first characterized an individual's strivings for a flawless existence as "The Tyranny of the Shoulds." Cultural emphasis on constant self-improvement has given us a belief that we must be able to handle any setback in life that comes our way. From our earliest years, we are taught that we should never compromise our aspirations, never settle for less. If we somehow wind up with less, we're accustomed to thinking that it's our fault — that we failed to do something we SHOULD have done.

The list of a woman's SHOULDS is often a long one. Ask yourself if you've ever been convinced that you should:

Never make any errors.

Be a perfect lover, mate, or daughter.

Serve as a flawless role model in your family.

Never give in to temper, fatigue, or a bad mood.

Practice perfect manners and self-control.

Most of us have a much longer list of SHOULDs than we're consciously aware of. Try this exercise to help you identify the ones that may be holding you back:

EXERCISE 5: "SHOULDING" YOURSELF
This is a long-term exercise. You will want to give it some deliberate attention and complete it over a few days' time. As you go about your

routines, monitor your thoughts for all the SOULDS that resound in your ears, and jot them down as you hear them.

When you have some quiet time, try to figure out where and when each SHOULD originated. Then ask yourself, *Is that source or value still relevant to my life now? Does completing that SHOULD still fulfill me? Or has it lost its necessity?* Draw a line through all the SHOULDs that no longer apply to the person you want to be now.

So far, we've dealt with needs and fears, if-onlys, unreasonable beliefs, and shoulds. There's just one more habit of learned helplessness that could be causing you to spin your wheels, and it's a major issue for many women. It's an intangible product of your own "inner space" that can sap your individuality, initiative, and energy, stranding you at one green light after another: You're still guided by the voices of people you should have left behind long ago.

You make decisions based on what you believe "they" believe, and continue to operate under the spell of perceived criticism from dead or estranged parents, dead spouses, ex-spouses, old enemies, even your high school guidance counselor. You are convinced that if you met them today they would tell you: "You didn't do it right, you should have accomplished more, done it better." The nagging perception that you are disappointing them is paralyzing.

Pretty soon, you're no longer able to distinguish between their thoughts and your own. The criticisms you heard earlier in life have become weapons you now deploy, and you have turned them against yourself. The result is a destructive running commentary in your own head, constantly undermining your vision and making green lights appear an angry red. I call this carping voice your "Negative Self-chatter."

GERALDINE

Geraldine was forty-three when she came to see me, with her negative self-chatter at such a high volume that she couldn't hear herself think. Her mother had died when she was in high school, after a long, painful bout with breast cancer. "I was with my mom when she took her last breath, while my father stayed at the office working. He couldn't even be there for her at the end. She must have felt so all alone."

Even though Geraldine had had a close relationship with her mother, they had fought constantly prior to the year her mother became terminally ill. "I was rebelling and she was dying. I felt we never got to resolve some issues or become closer. One of the last things she told me was that you can't depend on a man to be there when you need him."

Geraldine's father took over raising her and her younger brother. "I felt like Cinderella — doing cooking, cleaning, laundry, dishes — while they ate pizza and watched TV. My father was rarely home. When he was, he criticized me, saying I was just like my mother — lazy, unambitious. He said all I was good for was to get married."

After graduating from high school, Geraldine became a licensed beautician. She worked for several years at different salons but always harbored the wish to be her own boss. Geraldine never married because she never met anyone she felt could be "trusted to respect me." When Geraldine first came to see me, she was engaged to Mike, a sweet and sensitive guy, divorced, with custody of his two teenage children. She had met Mike the year her father died. She told me, "I'm scared that if I get married I will end up just like my mom: under some man's thumb, scrubbing floors and ironing shirts. I have a good job. I'm good — no, great — at what I do. So why ruin it by getting married?"

Since accepting Mike's engagement ring, Geraldine had suffered bouts of anxiety, but couldn't figure out why. She was scared. Mike had proposed many times and she had finally given in. "I love Mike and the kids, but in my brain I'm always thinking about what my father told me: All I'm good for is to get married. That's not what I want — just to get married. I want my own business."

Geraldine's negative self-chatter was a conflicting combination of the voices of both her parents. Although they were no longer alive, she internalized their mixed messages — her mother telling her not to rely on men, her father telling her that marriage was all she was good for. Neither voice was encouraging marriage. It was small wonder that Geraldine had trouble listening to her own heart.

We often dismiss our needs and aspirations because of negative self-chatter. This self-perpetuating narrative prevents us from listening to our inner selves. The overcompensating, responsible voice drowns out our true voice. Though the need for self-expression may be loud, the negative self-chatter can swell even louder in response.

When this happens to you, the stress that results can force you to throw away the only road map you have — yourself. You make sure no time is left to listen to that inner voice; you close the soundproof door, dismissing your desires as unimportant.

Only you can make sense of all this noise. To begin with, you'll need to separate the negative self-chatter from your own true inner voice. Then you need to silence the first, so you can learn to listen to the second. This is perhaps the single greatest accomplishment of Visionalysis, and the following series of exercises will guide you through it.

EXERCISE 6: TURNING OFF THE RADIO

To begin, tune in to your personal signal made up of the most negative self-chatter you can think of. Listen with a critical ear. Now, it's time to talk back! Challenge your chatter by asking yourself some questions: *What do you mean, I might fail? Exactly what will happen if I do not succeed?*

I'm serious. Write down all the possibilities you envision, — the worst possible scenarios and the consequences. Go ahead and construct a picture of what it will be like if your dire predictions come true. Include all the gory details. For instance, see yourself in that job you read about in the classifieds and daydreamed about having; then visualize all the possible catastrophes that might occur if you got it. Now ask yourself, *What are the chances these will come true?*

Next, consider — for each possibility on your list — whether the worst-case scenario would really be so tragic. I hope you are seeing now that your own daytime nightmares are what psychologist Dr. Albert Ellis calls "stupid thinking by a non-stupid person."

Next, take a piece of paper and write a letter to the sources of your negative self-chatter. Find holes in their reasoning; point out all the flaws you can see. Keep arguing until you win — only make sure the "you" with the positive attitude triumphs over "them."

Just because you've dealt with the negative self-chatter you're currently hearing, don't make the mistake of thinking you've silenced it forever. These critical inner voices are likely to speak up again promptly whenever you feel threatened or unsure. So you must learn to monitor them, and be ready to tune them out when necessary. Here are some typical forms of negative self-chatter to be on the lookout for:

I'll never be able to do that.

Nothing ever works out for me.

This will never work.

People will think I am crazy.

I'll spend a lot of money and once again end up with nothing.

What makes me think I could achieve this?

It will be just like the last time.

I've never been good at trying new things.

During the day, try to catch yourself in negative self-chatter — those internal, red-light sentences you repeat to yourself until you believe them. Dr. David D. Burns, in his book *Feeling Good*, categorizes these self-defeating thoughts as follows:

All-or-Nothing Thinking: If I can't do it perfectly, I won't do it. Here you eliminate potential choices because of some artificial consideration.

Overgeneralization: Believing one event is the standard for all; saying "I always" or "They never."

Discounting Positives: Looking for ways to change your positives to negatives.

Filtering: Focusing on the negatives and excluding the positives. This is what happens when someone compliments you and you tell yourself they must be mistaken.

Mind Reading: Being convinced that, despite what others tell you, you know what they are really thinking about you.

Fortune Telling: Predicting that things will not go well.

Magnification/Minimization: Distorting reality. Enlarging your fears.

Labeling: Believing that your actions and behavior are you — I'm stupid, etc.

By now you can see that negative self-chatter develops from fear. To have a chance at achieving a vision — even at this early stage of Visionalysis, before you know what that vision might be — you must define exactly what you fear. Before leaving this chapter, make sure you're satisfied that you've taken a leisurely Sunday drive past all the negative beliefs double-parked in your head. They will continue to clog traffic and prevent you from moving forward until you recognize them for what they are and give them a ticket.

At this point it is enough to have exposed your fears, if-onlys, unreasonable beliefs, shoulds, and negative self-chatter for what they are. Later, you'll learn how to watch out for them so you can drive around them. For now, you're ready to move on. It's time to treat yourself to a pre-trip inspection.

chapter 3

*G*ive Yourself an *E*motional *T*une-up

So far we've learned that if you stay parked in a pessimistic thinking zone, you avoid shifting your life into even the lowest low gear. You know the solution is to develop optimistic thinking. But first you need to determine which type of thinker you are right now.

EXERCISE 7: WHAT COLOR IS YOUR TRAFFIC LIGHT?
To see how you view yourself and the world, take the following short test. Respond by agreeing or disagreeing:

Regardless of how carefully I plan, something always goes wrong.

I never get a break.

I don't expect things to go my way.

The best strategy is to prepare for the worst.

I always look on the bright side.

When life gets tough, I know it won't last.

The best of my life is yet to come.

Even the most difficult times hold valuable lessons.

If you agree with the first four statements and disagree with the last four, you are a *red lighter* — someone who thinks pessimistically, whose radar screen is always scanning for red lights. If you disagree with the first four and agree with the last four, you are a *green lighter* — you scan optimistically. Obviously, you may not have totally agreed or disagreed with some of the statements. But this should give you a quick idea of how you generally respond to what happens to you. Are you fearful and defensive, seeing mostly the worst and negative side of things? Or do you immediately begin to problem-solve — to see how a liability can be turned into an asset or a lesson?

If you consider yourself to be optimistic, your road is automatically smoother. Accidents will happen. But when you know how to change your self-chatter from negative to positive, you're much better prepared to steer in the direction of the skid. Instead of freezing up when your quest seems to be sliding out of control, you will use your optimism to remain proactive, with the energy and focus you'll need to restore the mission to its original course.

This chapter is about testing your roadworthiness. You wouldn't set out on a long trip without giving your car a good going-over. Now is the time, before your vision quest begins, to understand what strengths you will bring to the challenge. Repeat to yourself the famous line from Shakespeare's *Hamlet*: "To thine own self be true." Visionalysis is about knowing yourself well enough to follow this excellent advice.

Enough about me, you might be thinking at this point. *What about all the people who matter in my life?* It's a good question, but I'll ask you to hold onto it just now — suspend it for a few more chapters. You need to negotiate first with yourself, then with others. You are responsible for creating your own happiness; you are not accountable for the total quality of someone else's life — no matter how much you love that person. When you help yourself, you help the person you care about. If you put down your own dreams and visions and say, *I can't do this because I will not be a good wife/mother/daughter/employee/committee member,* you are really saying, *I don't have much faith in my ideas or abilities.* And you know by now what that sounds like — just more negative self-chatter!

Don't worry: You don't have to issue ultimatums in your current relationships, or place a grenade between yourself and the matrix of people who comprise your life. What good would that do? Yes, you'd be free all right, and you might fulfill a lifelong dream of achievement, but with whom would you share it?

Before you can bring these people along on your journey, though, you have some important preparations to make alone.

LETTING THE INNER SELF OUT

As a woman begins to focus on herself, she is usually alone with her thoughts. She might pensively recall a journal she used to write in every day when she was younger, the poem she wrote at a turning point in her life, or the painting no other eyes have ever seen. She remains unaware that by continuing to suppress her individual energy, she sends herself the message that free expression — in a real sense who she is — is not important.

When women stifle their inner selves in this way, it is small wonder that they become distressed. Predictably, they look outside themselves to explain their unhappiness. Women have rarely been told that their personal thoughts are valuable or can be a means to solve their own problems. *What's wrong with me? I need a reality check from someone else. This may sound crazy, but . . . .* These are common feminine refrains.

> *"If I'm such a legend, then why am I so lonely?"*
>
> —JUDY GARLAND

For women who feel unfulfilled at this stage in their lives, it's a time of reckoning. Perhaps you were an industry trailblazer or you worked for years at a job you enjoyed . . . and now long just to be home and raise a family. Maybe you're like the lawyer who was vice president of a national brokerage house, then decided to move to Cape Cod to write a novel. Or like Leni Joyce, who parlayed her family inheritance from a defunct New England textile mill into a new business — weaving exotic fabrics by hand — that she heads up at the age of sixty-eight. Or like Ellen Kolton, the successful owner of a speaker's bureau who told the *Wall Street Journal* that her mother's death inspired her, at forty-six, to sell the business and become a patient advocate.

Many women are actively soul-searching, looking for new meaning and value in pursuits that are off the tracks they've followed for so long. Their angst is often misinterpreted or dismissed by their family and friends; yet these women are experiencing what their fathers, grandfathers, husbands, and boyfriends have been given societal permission to experience: mid-life adjusting.

But for most women, this mid-life recasting is not about having an affair with someone younger or desperately cramming in adventurous experiences; it's about redefining. Women are changing their "jobs" and their definition of happiness. Some are bailing out of high-pressure corporate positions to become independent consultants. Some apply the skills learned in business or at home to more spiritual endeavors like fund raising for a hospice, working in an AIDS center, teaching underprivileged children, or assisting in elder care.

> *"When work is a pleasure, life is a joy!*
> *When work is a duty, life is slavery."*
> —Maxim Gorky

Why are women more likely to seek the spiritual or socially useful redefinition, rather than one that brings them sensual gratification or success? Well, after all, being good has been a female prescription for centuries. It is often instilled in you early, with your family designating you as Daddy's good little girl. And it's good to be good, all right; deep down you know that you're happier when you "let your conscience be your guide," as the Blue Fairy admonished Pinocchio.

WHEN SHE WAS GOOD

But beware of insisting on a role for yourself that's too good to be true. When you are pursuing goodness, you'll want to make sure that it's for the right reasons. What would be a *wrong* reason for being good? A common one occurs when you are constantly seeking the approval of others — and as a result you feel ashamed if you are not perfectly competent in your work or perfectly unselfish in your motivations.

The Goodness Code, as Claudia Bepko and Jo-Ann Krestan called it in their book *Too Good for Her Own Good*, mandates that you be overly responsible — by doing for others, being responsible for others, and looking out primarily for the interests of others. In fulfilling this impossible edict, you unknowingly say to yourself that *your* desires, dreams, and goals should always take a back seat to theirs. This feeling of secondary importance only spurs you to focus more on others — whom you see as more worthy. You absorb their feelings, their needs, their anticipations, to fill the void, while your own feelings and visions are more deeply buried. When you ignore your own wants, you gain greater and greater skill at estimating and fulfilling the unmet needs of others.

The false assumption is that the more you do, the more valued you will be. You eventually come to believe that what you do for others is who you are. If you follow this prescription for goodness indefinitely, you may find yourself overdosed on the shame of having emotional needs. You will feel that no one knows who you really are, or sadly, you will assume that if others did know, they wouldn't find you lovable.

The Goodness Code has other precepts too many women live by:

Hypnotic Rule	Implication Women Follow Without Question
Be attractive.	A woman is as good as she looks.
Be a lady.	A good woman stays in control.
Be unselfish and of service.	A good woman lives to give.
Make relationships work.	A good woman loves first.
Be competent without complaint.	A good woman does everything well in silence.

Do any of these feel familiar? Chances are, you can already see some part of yourself in this goodness scenario. But just to make sure you see what I'm talking about, I'll tell you the story of Mary, one of my clients who fit the classic description of Daddy's good little girl — well into adulthood.

MARY

Mary had always felt pressured by her father to go into academics. He was a frustrated intellectual who dropped out of college during the Depression. He was determined that his daughter would not suffer the same fate.

Mary always did well in school, and she felt loved when she won academic awards. At an Ivy League school, Mary earned a PhD in English literature and started a college teaching career. Her conscientious, thorough work paid off and she was offered tenure after only three years. She focused her writing and research on scholarly topics, but she felt bored. That's when she came to see me, unsure of why she was so disillusioned when she had labored to be so good. "I've always wanted to write a novel," she told me, "but in the back of my mind, I felt my father wouldn't approve."

Mary struggled with the conflict between pleasing herself and incurring the disapproval of her father. She tried starting a novel several times, but her feelings of guilt and anxiety stopped her from going full steam ahead. She became increasingly unhappy with academic life. Finally, Mary realized she must forge ahead. "I knew something was wrong and if I spent the rest of my life trying to please my father and not myself, I would forever regret it."

Mary needed to change the way she viewed herself. She had to drive away from her fear of disapproval. It was essential for her to move out of the stage of hopelessness and regret, and pursue her long-held dream of writing a novel. She needed to forgo the security of the predictable success of her academic writing and pursue the unknown. But she was stalled because she couldn't seen to muster any optimism.

According to the late psychologist Dr. Abraham Maslow, who coined the term *self-actualization,* our "inner nature is not strong and overpowering and unmistakable like the instincts of animals. It is weak and delicate and subtle and easily overcome by habit, cultural pressure, and wrong attitudes toward it."

Mary's Visionalysis revealed the parental reason why she had stopped at a green light. As soon as she realized it, her accelerator came unstuck and she became her competent self again. It took two years for Mary to write her novel. For her, it was a gratifying milestone: "Even if it never gets published, I did it."

In perpetuating the strong influences of our childhood, we may empower others to control our destiny and give legitimacy to *their* hopes and dreams, not ours. You can break this spell with awareness, a game plan, perseverance, and support. Mary was able to change her thinking from her *passive voice* to her *active voice;* she changed her negative self-chatter from self-defeating to self-actualizing. No longer paralyzed by loyalty and obligation, she felt more content with her academic life and more competent to balance it with her fiction writing.

> *"Don't compromise yourself. You are all you've got."*
>
> —JANIS JOPLIN

If you're a mother who devotes every waking hour to doing everything for your children, you may often feel taken for granted. You may even be shocked at times by their lack of appreciation and by the disrespectful behavior you get in return. Not knowing that when you help yourself, you help them, you surmise that you are not doing enough. Your solution is to up the ante by doing more — which, of course, only perpetuates the problem. You become like a client of mine who said, "I couldn't give up all that giving behavior because it meant giving up the hope of being loved."

This vicious circle keeps going because of a shameful secret — you do not always want to be good. Sometimes you want to just check out, take a hot bath, kick your feet up, or read a novel. But you don't do this very often because, like the juggler at the circus, you desperately want to keep all your plates spinning in the air so everyone will keep clapping. Ironically, when you avoid owning up to this desire not to always be good, you become too good for your own good.

That secret may be your salvation. If you can face it without plunging into ever-greater feats of goodness, you will at last become genuinely good — to yourself. Learning to resist your urge to be perfectly good frees you to behave in ways you yourself define as good — according to your own values. And that way lies happiness!

> *"Happiness can grow in any soil, live in any condition. It defies environment. It comes from within; it is the revelation of the depths of the inner life as light and heat proclaim the sun from which they radiate. Happiness consists not of having, but of being; not of possessing, but of enjoying. It is the warm glow of the heart at peace with itself. Happiness is the soul's joy in the possession of the intangible. Happiness is paradoxical because it may coexist with total sorrow and poverty. It is the gladness of the heart, rising superior to all conditions."*
> —WILLIAM GEORGE JORDAN, FROM JOY MILLER, *My Holding You Up Is Holding Me Back*

If any of the scenarios I've discussed so far sound like you, then your next question must be: *What can I do about it?* That is what this book is about; I want to show you how to investigate the sources of your discontent and reevaluate your current position, so that you can proceed to design what Gail Sheehy refers to as your "second adulthood." If your first adulthood was about pleasing others, this next one can be about reconnecting with your long-latent dreams and relating to the people in your life in a new, more balanced and meaningful way. Sounds better, doesn't it? This is a time to tune in to your needs.

> *"It is not easy to find happiness in ourselves, and it is not possible to find it elsewhere."*
> —AGNES REPPLIER

EXERCISE 8: JUST HOW HAPPY ARE YOU?

Let's get a feel for where you are on the happiness scale. This is not a system that compares you with others, but an internal meter that monitors your personal levels of satisfaction. Answer the following questions, keeping track of your responses in your notebook, as simply a, b, or c:

1. When I look at my life so far I feel:
   (a) it has been more good than bad;
   (b) it has been more bad than good;
   (c) it has been unbelievably good.

2. At the end of most days I usually feel:
   (a) I could have done more;
   (b) I'm glad that's over;
   (c) I am satisfied with how it went.

3. When I look in the mirror, I:
   (a) think my face and body are okay;
   (b) see a lot of shortcomings;
   (c) am pleased with my image.

4. I wish every day were:
   (a) longer, so I could sleep later;
   (b) shorter because I'm so bored most of the time;
   (c) longer because there are so many things I want to do.

5. If I read about violence, I:
   (a) feel lucky it didn't involve me;
   (b) resolve to go out as little as possible;
   (c) consider that most news reports are bad; that good news is also all around us.

6. When I wake up, I:
   (a) accept what's coming up that day;
   (b) am mad I couldn't sleep longer;
   (c) am eager to start the day.

7. My friends are:
   (a) okay to be with but nothing special;
   (b) not as interesting as I wish they were;
   (c) terrific people I'm lucky to know.

8. I would describe myself as:
   (a) just like everyone else;
   (b) not as valuable as some other people;
   (c) a unique person with attributes to offer.

9. When I gain weight, I:
   (a) accept it as normal that my weight will fluctuate at times;
   (b) realize it will probably remain because I have trouble losing weight;
   (c) immediately start an exercise and diet regime.

10. When I am feeling depressed, I:
    (a) know it will pass;
    (b) think it may linger for a long time;
    (c) do something for myself to break the spell.

Give yourself one point for each (a) answer; no points for each (b) answer; and two points for each (c) answer.

If you scored 14-20 points: Good for you! You are generally a positive person who handles life's ups and downs with flexibility and optimism. You will find it relatively easy to achieve your vision.

If you scored 7-13 points: You're satisfied but not enthused about your life. Your attitudes waver between positive and negative. You'll need to work on transforming your negative self-chatter to optimistic, hopeful thought, so you can pursue your goals with more vigor.

If you scored 0-6 points: You see rain instead of rainbows a lot of the time. Mostly red and yellow lights appear when you look down the road to your future. We can turn them to green; but it will take some effort, and you must pay close attention to each step in this book — Visionalysis, Visioneering, Visioncrafting, and Visionavigating. Don't move on to the next step until you're sure you are ready. I want you to succeed!

ACCENTUATE THE POSITIVE

How can I predict so confidently that high scorers in this exercise will have an easier time through the vision process? After all, I have no way of knowing what your circumstances are, or what may happen to you tomorrow or next year. But we know this: Optimists are only temporarily affected by negative life events, even tragedies. When a setback occurs, a grouchy person tends to brood about it, while the upbeat individual's positive outlook returns quickly. Studies of happiness around the world have found that money makes little difference, except in cases of extreme poverty. Lottery winners were no happier a year later than before they won. Education, marriage, and family do not correlate reliably with contentment, and are minor factors compared with a person's inner sense of well-being. Hollywood star Christopher Reeve is a case in point: After a terrible injury to his spinal cord when he fell from his horse, his strong, confident spirit found a way to rebound.

Studies of 1,500 pairs of twins by behavioral geneticist Dr. David T. Lykken of the University of Minnesota found that 50 percent of a person's sense of well-being is determined by genes, while the other half results from life's vagaries. According to Lykken, professionals were no happier than laborers, and those who had Ph.D.s were no happier than those other Ph.D.s — post-hole diggers.

According to the leading psychologist in happiness research, Dr. David G. Myers of Hope College, the author of *The Pursuit of Happiness*, the following attributes enable a person to be happy:

A fit and healthy body

Realistic goals and expectations

Positive self-esteem

Feelings of control

Optimism

Outgoingness

Supportive friendships that facilitate companionship and confiding

A socially intimate, sexually warm, equitable primary relationship

Challenging work and active leisure, punctuated by adequate rest and retreat

A faith that entails communal support, purpose, acceptance, outward focus, and hope

Look at Myers's list of attributes. How many apply to you? What resolutions can you make to bring the others into your life?

Myers's recipe for well-being includes, in his words, a "mix of ample optimism to provide hope, a dash of pessimism to prevent complacency, and enough realism to discriminate those things we can control from those we cannot." Myers further explains, "Well-being is found in renewal of disciplined life-styles, committed relationships, and the receiving and giving of acceptance. To experience deep well-being is to be self-confident yet unselfconscious, self-giving yet self-respecting, realistic yet hope-filled." Myers says we function best with "modest self-enhancing illusions" that can help us overcome our doubts.

HAPPINESS IS . . .

People come to my office with nagging doubts about who they are and where they are in their lives. When I ask them what they would like to do if they could, they routinely say, "I don't know." That's okay, because there are no right or wrong answers. In fact, it is surprising when any of us *do* know; we have many more options and opportunities than our parents had. We even have the luxury of focusing on ourselves, unlike those in generations before ours whose primary goal was survival.

This book is about exploring the myriad possibilities available to you today and tomorrow, then zeroing in on a specific goal. But you won't get far on such an expedition unless you are well-equipped with self-knowledge. Here's an exercise to help you discover what happiness means to you.

EXERCISE 9: WHAT DOES A GREEN LIGHT LOOK LIKE?

Write answers to the following questions in your notebook. Keep in mind that this is private; you have no one else's expectations to live up to.

What carries meaning for you?

What moves you to tears of joy?

When was the last time you felt most gratified, as if something you did was really worthwhile?

When was the last time you exclaimed, "Yessss!" or couldn't wait to engage in an activity or read about something, or share with others what aroused your enthusiasm?

What do you do for play?

What are you doing when the time just seems to fly by?

What kind of undertaking makes you feel anxious and empowered at the same time?

What personal, social, or spiritual values have meaning for you?

What personal hidden aspects are screaming to get out and express themselves? If you had a day to spend exactly as you wished, what would you choose to do?

Whom do you admire or envy?

Whose life do you see as ideal? Why?

What do you daydream about?

In which areas of your life do you feel capable, incapable?

What do you expect from yourself?

What do you want to be important in your life?

This Visionalysis of your sources of joy may cause you to reevaluate what makes you happy — or what *might* make you happy — that you may not have considered before. Remember Carol's story, at the beginning of this section? Her Visionalysis revealed that the ingredients for her happiness were already present, in the blended family made up of her mother, her husband, and her stepson. Once she realized this, she could take steps to transform her family into a functioning, healthy whole.

How do we define happiness, anyway? How does each of us pursue it? Poets, philosophers, and gurus have debated this for centuries. For some happiness lies in having money; for some, having power. For others, it's found in nurturing relationships, or moral and spiritual pursuits. Some naturally gravitate toward friendship and family (nurturing), while others are drawn to contribute to society through work (achieving).

> *". . . there are two ways to meet life; you may refuse to care until indifference becomes a habit, a defensive armor, and you are safe — but bored. Or you can care greatly, and live greatly — till life breaks you on its wheel."*
>
> —DOROTHY CANFIELD FISHER

True happiness, then, is individually defined, but the common denominator seems to be a sense of well-being. Today more than ever, women have replaced and expanded the traditional measures of success (money, fame, and power) with more internal values. They place greater value on relationships (with family, friends, customers, coworkers, mentors, professional organizations) and seek happiness and fulfillment through personal meaning.

According to a University of Michigan national survey, three out of five respondents who reported having personal control in their lives said they were "very happy." Psychologists have a term that expresses being in control: the *internal locus of control.* It is the essential ingredient for the experience of well-being. People who possess an internal locus of control are better adapters to stress, do better academically, and live more happily. Control comes with confidence, and confidence comes with success — the sort of success that, like happiness, is individually and internally defined.

The key to achieving your defined success is to actively manage where you are heading. This means driving with both hands on the wheel, and not fiddling with the rearview mirror. Remember, the way to achieve control is to practice — even if you have to do it scared. My goal is to get you mentally ready for each practice run before you attempt it.

If you're like most women, being liked, affirmed, and encouraged by those around you is especially important to your happiness. Extroverts — people who actively seek out the company of others — obviously are likely to enjoy greater social support and well-being. In one study, Purdue University students were instructed to keep track of their daily mood swings. The results of the study showed that those scoring high as extroverts consistently rated their days' experiences as happier, even if they encountered some unhappy moments.

So, as we can see, happiness involves having a positive self-image, an internal locus of control, optimism, and an outgoing personality style. If these traits don't naturally apply to you, it will help if you go through the motions anyway — if you "fake it until you make it." Thinking more positively makes you feel more optimistic; in turn you act on these feelings. To paraphrase Billy Crystal's character Fernando on Saturday Night Live, if you think "mahvelous," you will act "mahvelous."

Scientific studies support this notion. In one experiment, psychologists taught depressed people to smile — even when they had to fake it. Once the smiling muscles were activated, people reported feeling happier and less sad. So the proof is there that if you do it, you can feel it.

Other behavioral studies show that how you walk can affect your self-confidence. Swinging your arms and taking big strides lead to more self-confidence and a greater sense of well-being. Greta Garbo was once observed entering a movie theater in the pitch dark one night: Although no one could see her face, she was recognized because of her noble carriage — long strides, with chin up and waist forward in a proud stride. Just changing a couple of things about the way you walk — like looking up and ahead — has amazing consequences for how you feel about yourself. You too can display confidence by striding proudly — even if you don't feel it.

> *"Happiness depends less on having things than on our attitude toward the things we have."*
> —DR. DAVID G. MYERS OF HOPE COLLEGE, AUTHOR OF *The Pursuit of Happiness*

Another way to banish unhappiness is to do what your grandmother would have advised: Count your blessings. I mean it. Take out a piece of paper and list everything you feel or have ever felt grateful for in your life. Go crazy — include everything that turned out better than you expected. Recall everyone who has helped you — those you asked for help and those you didn't. What you'll discover is that you can't be regretful or bitter while you are feeling appreciative. They're mutually exclusive.

Finally, if you hang around confident, upbeat people, it will rub off. Just as misery loves company, exuberance is contagious.

> *"The greatest discovery of my generation is that human beings, by changing their inner attitudes of their minds, can change the outer aspects of their lives."*
>
> —WILLIAM JAMES

In this chapter, you've learned the importance of making your own happiness a priority. And you've discovered ways to nurture that happiness and well-being in yourself. There's just one more important point we must discuss before we can proceed toward envisioning your route to the rest of your life. And that's how to avoid letting any misguided detours in your past catch up with you.

chapter 4

Don't Get Hit from Behind

Although we know it's futile, we waste enormous energy punishing ourselves by reliving our mistakes. We ruminate over failures, hoping to return to do it right this time around. Despite knowing the adage about 20/20 hindsight, we still hopelessly cling to opportunities passed over, adventures missed. Interrupting this pattern is vital to your progress. Scan this list to see whether any of the following regrets apply to you. Then we'll address what you can do about them.

I wish I had put my family before my career more often.

I wish I had balanced my family and work life better.

If I had known this job entailed this much work, I would not have taken it.

If I had known this mortgage would become such a burden, I would have settled for a smaller house.

I haven't lived up to my potential.

I missed the opportunity to pursue my dreams when I was young. I've wasted a lot of time in my life.

I wish I had taken more risks.

I wish I had spent more time with my kids while they were growing up.

I wish I had chosen some other place to live.

I wish I had been less reluctant to try new experiences.
I wonder what I might have done with my life if I had it to do over.
I fantasize about how successful I might have been.
I wish I had been more impulsive.
I wish I had followed my intuition more in planning my life.
I wish I had put more effort into my education.
I wish I could express myself better in all my relationships.

Do you see that giving in to this kind of wishful thinking amounts to taking a trip right back to the Land of If-Only? Regret keeps you uncertain whether you should go in reverse or move forward. Lamenting implies personal failure, which makes you feel that what you have done so far is not valuable.

The choices you made in the past have shaped your life today. You don't need to apologize. Perhaps looking back, you might have chosen someone else as a mate, pursued a different career, decided not to have a family, lived in a different part of the country or the world, backpacked through Europe. But you didn't. Remember, you still learned something of value from your experiences even if they brought you pain, such as a divorce or a career failure. You must mourn the loss, and then go on.

Sadly, the regret I most often hear from women in mid-life centers on an early decision to be a homemaker. They feel this renders them less valuable in today's society. To me, this constitutes a great injustice — the notion that creating a healthy home and raising children is something less than an honorable endeavor. I get very angry when I hear others degrade a woman's choice to be a wife and mother. These judgmental people are short-sighted and perhaps are affected by the latest social trends. In the larger scheme of the advancement of the species, homemaking is a most valuable vocation.

Whatever if-onlys may lie on the road behind you, it's a fatal error to spend your valuable time ruminating about what wasn't. Instead, focus your thinking on what can be. Self-pity will only hold you back. It's okay to feel sad about lost opportunities, but it's not productive to let them catch up with you at every crossroads you encounter.

Sure, you might have married a more sensitive lover, not married so young, chosen to go on to graduate school, not dropped out of college, finished high school, had no kids or more kids, not worked. Don't be like the fisherman who only dwells on the big one that got away. Don't waste your vitality; you'll need it where you're going — on to your second adulthood.

"Life is either a daring adventure or nothing."
—HELEN KELLER

Often life just happens to us — as John Lennon said, "when we're busy making other plans." And this might be an important part of your story. But now is the time for compassion and self-forgiveness. Your future second adulthood is filled with hope. Don't get bogged down trying to rewrite the past exactly as you would have liked it to have been scripted. Look instead to create a new book, with new chapters, perhaps filled with whatever was lacking in your past.

DON'T LOOK BACK

Psychological research shows that we tend to regret those things we didn't get to do, more than the things we didn't do right. For example, Dr. Nancy K. Schlossberg and Susan Porter Robinson demonstrated in their book *Going to Plan B* that many people regret in their life what she calls "non-events," such as the college that was not attended or the child not conceived or the career never attempted. My conclusion: The road you choose not to take will cause you much more pain than taking a wrong turn.

"Two roads diverged in a wood, and I —
I took the one less traveled by,
And that has made all the difference."
—ROBERT FROST

The biblical story of Sodom and Gomorrah teaches us a lesson about looking back and its consequences: God decided to destroy the cities of Sodom and Gomorrah because the citizens had become pleasure-seekers. Since Lot was a righteous man, angels told him to gather his possessions and leave the city without looking back. As Lot and his family reached the gates of the city, Lot's wife glanced back longingly and was turned into a pillar of salt. She had wanted one last look at what she was leaving behind. The salt is a symbol of her tears.

Of course, if you have regrets, you won't turn into a pillar of salt — that doesn't have to be your "lot in life." But the Bible story reminds us of the dangers of focusing too long on the past.

MINDING OUR OTHERS

Allowing others to define who you are — and how good a person you are — is another traffic circle of regrets you can find yourself driving around and around. Consider whether the following statements apply to you:

I wish I'd spent more time with good friends.

I wish I hadn't done what was expected of me.

I've made too many sacrifices for others.

I wish I were more independent, not so reliant on others.

I've adopted other people's values instead of my own.

Other people kept me from realizing my potential.

I wish I didn't accept other people's problems as my own.

I wish I'd chosen my partner more wisely.

I wish I'd been a better parent.

I wish I'd been a better daughter.

I wish I had a more satisfying love relationship.

I wish I'd been a better wife.

I wish I'd been a better employee.

I wish I didn't need others' approval.

I wish other's opinions didn't mean so much to me.

These past-tense if-onlys are just as insidious and self-defeating as the first list — even more so, because now you've involved other people in your regrets. If any of these statements are true for you, try putting them in the future tense instead — I won't accept other people's problems as my own; I will be a better worker. Do you see how this conversion of regret to resolve can make the road ahead of you that much more accessible?

Can you think of other ways that an optimistic outlook can convert the red lights of your past to the green lights of your future?

> *"Things do not change; we change."*
> —HENRY DAVID THOREAU

The seeds of regret are sown in our childhood. Research with over eight hundred children from kindergarten through high school showed that adult regret stems from our early emotional setbacks. Aversions to risk-taking that emerge in adulthood are ways to avoid challenging ourselves with equally painful experiences.

If you find yourself habitually glancing backward at what might have been, you need to — forgive me if I offend you — get over yourself. The anger you feel is a learned response; you can unlearn it. You can steer in a direction away from this traffic circle of regret. By examining your dissatisfaction honestly, you will find that these complaints have become a buffer to protect you from uncertainty, randomness, and unpredictability.

Regret comes from not having tried. A nagging sense of missing your exit may indicate that you've lost sight of what matters most to you — whether it's taking nature walks, watching stand-up comedy, spending more time with family, sledding, visiting art galleries, completing an assignment, closing a sale, or serving customers well. Try now to reach for things that keep the rest of your life humming.

Remember, life involves trade-offs; perhaps the choices you made earlier didn't express your true beliefs and values. Just think of it this way — concessions you made were a learning experience. But you stand to lose a whole lot more if you don't pursue your vision now.

> *"If you do what you have always done,*
> *you'll get what you've always gotten."*
> —ANONYMOUS

CANDACE

Candace, at fifty-one, was to all appearances a highly successful attorney. Raised in Pittsburgh in an upper-middle-class family, she had always done well in school. Her parents, both lawyers, made it clear early in Candace's life that they expected she would follow in their footsteps by going to law school. So she did.

After a failed marriage and no children, Candace came to see me complaining of anxiety attacks that came on out of the blue. She was *helpless* to control them, and so she felt *hopeless*.

As we talked about her family and her parents, Candace became depressed. "I love my mom and dad very much but I wish they had let me do what I wanted with my life." As we used Visionalysis to explore her discontent, Candace came to realize that she had chosen law for all the wrong reasons: "I did it for them — not for me. It's not that I hate practicing law but I have discovered that my interests now lie elsewhere."

She also said, "It's not that I haven't tried to adapt. First I tried criminal law because my parents said it would be lucrative. I didn't like it, so after ten years of defending many guilty people, I tried family law. That's when I discovered I really like helping parents cope with their kids as they go through a divorce. Now I'm miserable for all the right reasons. This is my real calling." When I heard Candace say that last sentence, although her destination still was not clear, I knew she had located her individual compass — a way to focus on her hopes for the future rather than her regrets about the past.

Once we had unveiled these fundamental facts of her life, we went to work on Candace's vision process. She decided to go back to school to get her doctorate. She found out what courses were required, then proceeded to qualify herself to teach adult education classes at the college level. Today she is a professor of family studies at her local university.

RESETTING THE ODOMETER

Changing how you feel about regrets is a challenge; the negative feelings and painful thoughts are stubbornly ingrained. Each time you think about the person, occurrence, or opportunity lost, you replay all the same arguments with yourself and choke on the same emotions. Human nature and habit encourage us to cling tenaciously to whatever is most familiar, even if it is painful.

I know; changing is easier said than done. The following exercise will provide you with a handy device for intercepting and short-circuiting your regrets and resetting them in a forward direction.

EXERCISE 10: THE REARVIEW MIRROR
Think about the parts of your past that you can't seem to leave behind. Then ask yourself these questions:

> How strongly do I feel about this regret?
>
> Has the intensity of the feeling changed over time?
>
> If it has increased, why?
>
> If it has decreased, is it still worth the emotional energy I am spending on it?
>
> Do I blame myself for what did or did not happen?
>
> Is my regret realistic or was what happened inevitable?
>
> If I am responsible, what change can I make to avoid a recurrence?
>
> Can I think of anything I can do to soften my regret?

This last question does not mean you must take action to correct an old error; it includes forgiving yourself for making a mistake, promising yourself you will do whatever is possible never to let it happen again, or crafting a more acceptable plan for the next time. Or it might involve reaching out and changing the way you relate to the world: making amends with someone, taking more risks, spending more time with your friends, children, or grandchildren.

You can apply this same process to those less specific longings that sometimes haunt you — the vague sense that there is something you need in order to make your life complete.

Ask yourself:

> How strongly do I still long for this lost opportunity?
>
> Is the intensity of my feeling realistic?
>
> Would things have really been that much better had they worked out differently? How wonderful or detrimental might it have been if this had come to pass?
>
> Was the outcome within my control?
>
> Did I have valid reasons for choosing not to take that path? Did some other good things come from *not* following my desire? Did I know, at the time, that I would have regrets?

Can I do anything presently to diminish or ameliorate my regret? Perhaps I can pursue the lost opportunity in my spare time, or do some modified version — or maybe take up the dream now.

What triggers my feelings of regret? Is there an underlying problem that needs to be resolved first, before I can pursue a missed chance?

Will identifying another dream, and going after it, alleviate this longing?

Feeling sorry about things that might have been is like any other counterproductive emotion: Although powerful and difficult to erase, it's like a tough stain that can be removed if you apply the right solution to break it down. Spend time figuring out how to rub out this regret from your life. Maybe it's time now to forgive yourself for what may not have been a perfect choice.

Then make a plan, broken down into small sequential steps. Proceed step by step. Don't expect results tomorrow; instead, work slowly and steadily. Regardless of what you lament, the final goal is to become more mindful — at peace with yourself. It's well worth the effort to feel resolved about your past, so that it doesn't slam into you from behind while you're waiting at the light.

> *"It is a rule of life that when one door closes, another door always opens. Let us not, therefore, mourn so much for the losses behind the closed door, that we miss the opportunities waiting for us beyond the newly opened door."*
>
> —ANDRÉ GIDE

YOUR INNER LIMITS

There's another habit from your old life that you'll need to shake before you can move on to Visioneering: the tendency to indulge in self-limiting beliefs. These are perceptions of yourself that may or may not still hold true, and that impede your freedom of movement. Turn these self-imposed red lights to green by holding in your mind both the past and future versions of your vision: see yourself before, and then after.

In a weight-loss center where I was a consultant, when a woman enrolled for the first time, we took a picture of her. When she reached her goal weight, we took a follow-up snapshot. She could then see herself before and after.

In your case, of course, I'm talking about shedding beliefs, not pounds. Your "before" snapshot would include your pessimistic, self-limiting beliefs. The follow-up shot would reveal the optimistic non-limiting beliefs hiding under all that pessimism. Old beliefs — your red lights — might be impressions like "I'm too old" or "I'm not smart enough." The corresponding green light might be "Wisdom comes with age."

When the traffic in your head gets too congested, one way to direct your feelings from helplessness into hopefulness is to switch off any negative self-chatter as soon as you hear it. A technique for accomplishing this is called "Thought Stopping."

EXERCISE 11: BLOCK THAT THOUGHT!
First, write down your red lights — any thoughts that block your progress, all the reasons why you believe you can't do what you want. Look both within yourself and at outside influences — there's no end to the limiting beliefs you can come up with! Here are some examples to help you get started:

Red Lights from Within	Red Lights from Without
I'm not smart enough.	My family will be mad.
I'm not pretty enough.	We can't afford it.
I'm too old.	My marriage won't survive.
I don't deserve it.	He'll never agree.
I made my bed so I have to lie in it.	Who'll be there when the kids get home?
I never went to college.	Who do you think you are?
My idea is not valuable, or workable.	I don't have a car.

Red Lights from Within	Red Lights from Without
I'm biting off more than I can chew.	But Mom...
Why would they hire me?	Is it really worth upsetting people?
I'll look stupid.	How can I work and go to school?
I'll get sick.	I don't have the time.
Can I really make it?	
It's too hard for me.	
What a dumb idea!	
I'll be left all alone.	
Things never work out for me.	
I always seem to screw up.	
I'm not being a good person.	
I'm not being nice.	

Take any one of these sentences and adapt it to your situation. For example, if you're considering returning to school for courses or a degree, you might be concerned about the difficulty of the assignments. You might even say to yourself, *I'm too old and I won't remember what I read.*

Now go to a private place. Close your eyes and say that sentence to yourself. When you have clearly heard it, yell "Stop!" out loud. You will notice that the limiting belief immediately leaves your mind. The reason is simple: You can't hold two thoughts in your mind simultaneously. You can't yell "Stop!" and conduct negative self-chatter at the same time.

What you may notice, now that you have learned how to Thought Stop, is that pessimistic thoughts will fight back. They might even initially increase in frequency. Don't forget, they have found a comfortable home in your heart and mind for a long time and are not about to vacate easily. But you can hand them an eviction notice. Of course, it's not practical to go around yelling "Stop!" out loud. So it's okay to yell it to yourself instead.

Now go through your red light list, say each item to yourself, then practice yelling "Stop!" When you catch yourself thinking of ways to put yourself down during the day, yell "Stop!" Remember, our beliefs control our feelings — and these direct our actions.

Once you have mastered the thought-stopping technique, you can move on to replacing these negative thoughts with more optimistic ones. Go back to your list of progress-blocking sentences and personal put-downs and add what cognitive psychologists call reframing. Using the example we chose earlier—*I'll never remember what I read*—you might change this sentence to *Even though I am older now than when I last went to school, my experience and wisdom will help me do well.* Practice replacing the old red light with a new green light by closing your eyes and repeating an encouraging sentence. After a while, with enough of these repetitions, your positive thoughts will flow more freely. Your mind won't want to go through all the hard work of thought-stopping, and the optimistic sentences will begin to come up automatically.

To keep yourself in the habit of looking forward, you can rid your self-chatter of certain phrases that reduce your horsepower. These, too, can be thought-stopped and replaced. Here are some to practice:

Red Lights	Green Lights
I can't . . .	I will decide whether to . . .
I should . . .	If I want to I can . . .
I had nothing to do with it.	I take responsibility for it.
It's a problem.	It's a challenge I can meet.
I'm never finished.	I just took one more step toward my goal.
This is a struggle.	Nothing worthwhile is easy.
I hope I can.	I know I can.
If only I had . . .	Next time, I will.
But what if . . .	If this happens, I'll . . .
This is a catastrophe.	This is not a national crisis; I can handle it.

As you can see, the green light column puts you in control; the red light left column keeps everyone and everything else in charge.

Another way to remold your negative thoughts to positive ones is to argue with them. This is called *disputation.* You can do it alone, but I suggest you practice it with someone else who has your best interests at heart. Set aside around twenty minutes, and explain to your friend, colleague, or mate that you need their help to challenge some negative internal thinking.

EXERCISE 12: GET INTO AN ARGUMENT
Pick an item, any item, from your list of self-defeating red lights, and tell the other person to be you. Have that individual advocate the position of your red light. Your task will be to combat those negative contentions by taking the optimistic approach. The following are some strategies to help you win the argument with your "self":
Use facts, just as if you were presenting evidence in court, to contradict the accusation.

Look for alternative explanations; practically nothing happens for only one reason.

Here's a sneaky one: Agree with your "adversary"; concede that the statement is true. Then attack from another angle. What difference does it make? Are the implications all that devastating, or can you accomplish your goal anyway?

Again, agreeing with the stated fact, dispute by arguing that there is no reason why your red light needs to stay true.

An additional tactic is to question the relevancy of the original statement. Even if true, does it have to be addressed immediately in order to proceed with your overall plan?

You can also do this alone, if necessary. Simply write out every contradictory response you can come up with, using the examples above as a guide. Remember, these suggestions are just to get you started; I'll bet you can come up with some very convincing disputes of your own.

> *"We are what we think. All that we are arises with our thoughts. We make our world."*
>
> —BUDDHA

As you continue to change your red lights to green, you will see setbacks as temporary, not permanent. You can tell yourself — and believe — that you are not stuck in an endless traffic jam, but have alternative avenues for escape. Such an attitude realignment is vital; ability and motivation alone are insufficient to drive you to your goal.

You must have optimism to change your current status and bring your dreams to fruition.

SUMMARY: VISIONALYSIS

You're ready to move on to Visioneering — one giant step closer to your new life. But first, let's go over some of the concepts you've mastered in your Visionalysis. They'll definitely come in handy on the journey ahead:

1. Learned helplessness — the giving-up response that women adopt when they don't get what they need — leads directly to hopelessness. One way to cure learned helplessness is by teaching yourself to take responsibility and even some risks.
2. If you think optimistically, you'll have a better chance of success and an easier time spotting green lights.
3. Needs and fears, if-onlys, unreasonable beliefs, shoulds, and negative self-chatter are all bad habits of learned helplessness that could cause you to spin your wheels.
4. Beware of insisting on a role for yourself that's too good to be true. When you are pursuing goodness, you'll want to make sure that it's for the right reasons.
5. Making your own happiness a priority is vital if you want to be a positive presence in the lives of others.
6. Through techniques like thought-stopping and disputation, the red lights of regret and limiting beliefs can be changed to green.

part

VISIONEERING

chapter 5

*S*he Who
*H*esitates
*I*s Lost

LIBBY

Libby had always been career-driven, even as a child. Little did she know that years later, when she was in her late forties, her career-mindedness would dramatically change her life.

Libby started her first business — as a baby-sitter/camp director — at age twelve. "Yes — a *business*. I knew how to raise children — I had eight brothers and sisters to look after, while my parents drank themselves practically to death." Libby started her own summer camp for the neighborhood kids. "I realized that all the kids came to play with my brothers and sisters anyway, and I was always working as the referee, nurse, mother, camp counselor, and lunch-maker. So why not get paid for it?"

She made up flyers, gave them to everyone within a three-block radius, and soon made money. She hired friends her age to help out and gave them a part of the fee. "Even then, I knew what I was doing. It came out of necessity. I can't say I chose it, but there it was."

When Libby reached her junior year in high school, she began investigating colleges and scholarships. "I wasn't a brain, just a hard worker with *lots* of motivation. I wanted to get away from home and out of my family. Education and practical experience seemed the only way." Libby's father worked at a series of odd jobs: janitor, night watchman, gardener, and handyman. Libby's mother supplemented the family income by working as a waitress, receptionist, grocery store bagger, and other service positions. Libby decided early, "I didn't want that for myself."

No one encouraged Libby, or discouraged her from having a career or doing well in school. "It was like I didn't exist except to help out at home. I was only as good as I was useful. I didn't cause my parents any problems at school, so that was good enough for them." Unable to get the help or resources she needed to apply to an out-of-town school, Libby got a work-study scholarship at the local college. She lived at home and "worked and studied twenty-five hours a day. I still had to help out at home; at school I had to get good grades to keep the scholarship, and work in the school cafeteria bussing tables. It was the most disgusting job. I swore I'd never work around food again."

Libby had very little time available for a social life. "I think I had one date in my four years in college. No — I had two — with the same guy; he wanted me to write his papers for him. I thought, what do I need this for?" Libby majored in business, specializing in marketing.

After college, Libby took a job with a major kitchen cabinet company. "I knew kitchens, houses, anything for the home. I had managed a whole family — plus two dependent, childlike parents. I understood what kinds of cabinets, designs, appliances people needed." After a while, Libby's job expanded to include marketing, advertising, and scouting and developing new territories. She stayed with the company for over twenty years, ultimately bringing home a six-figure income.

By the time she was in her forties, Libby had grown restless. "My life didn't seem to move. I dated, had boyfriends, but no one to shout about. I didn't put much faith in relationships. When I had them, they went okay — not great, but okay. I dated lots of different men, but was never really in love."

She felt her personal life was stalled. She knew she didn't want children — her own or anyone else's. "I'd had it with child-rearing. My own siblings were a mess — lots of drugs and alcohol abuse. None of them went to college. They were in and out of jobs. I was the only one who made it out."

Libby had good friends and a social network, but felt frustrated. "I was embarrassed to tell anyone I was unhappy. I was healthy, made lots of money, and was not desperately lonely. I wouldn't have minded if a man came into my life, but I wasn't looking either. Yet, I was not feeling content."

When Libby turned forty-seven, she became very depressed. "I had never been depressed before. To this day I can't really explain it. I was always a person of action. I blamed it on hormones, but I think it was just life catching up with me." Libby had assumed she would just go on, one year after the next, making money, having friends, being healthy and happy. "I didn't know where this restlessness was coming from."

Actually, Libby's situation is not unusual. As men and women reach mid-life and want something different, they look around for a change of pace. Libby was an achiever, and by the time she passed the twenty-year mark with her company, she felt bored. She felt she "had done it all," going as far as she could with the company. She wanted something more. For the first time in her life she felt "lost."

After ruminating for over a year, Libby came to see me. I was struck by how embarrassed she was to admit she wanted help. And she was even more ashamed to confess that she was clueless about which direction to take. She was unaccustomed to feeling out of control. She was frightened, and felt *hopeless*.

Her natural optimism, which had served her so well, was plummeting. Week after week during Visionalysis, Libby denied that she was uneasy about her career. At that point, she was more afraid of change than she was unhappy. Sometimes a person has to wait until the pain of her unhappiness is greater than her fears. When Libby reached her "halfway birthday mark," she panicked. In her mind she felt "almost fifty — and over the hill." The only feeling she could identify was the urge to "act fast on something."

BACK TO THE DRAWING BOARD

Now that her motivation was greater than her fears, Libby was willing to explore new ideas — to go Visioneering. This is basically a design process, a matter of sketching out a road map that charts a possible course to a feasible goal. During the Visioneering phase, all options are still open before you. The point is to get the strongest possible indication of the direction in which you want your dreams to lead you.

To do this, Libby brainstormed, writing down "crazy ideas," as she called them. She knew she was good at business, and she determined that she wanted to stay in a business-related venture. "That was an important step for me. I was scared to death something bad was going to jump out of my head — like maybe I wanted to be a ballerina."

Reaffirming that being in business was the way she wanted to head made her feel calm, and, most importantly, more *optimistic*. "I knew that somewhere out there was a business I wanted to be a part of."

Libby wrote down all the things she liked and was interested in. I told her not to worry about a specific company or job title for now. "Just brainstorm," I told her; "list your pleasures, fantasies, likes and dislikes, and skills." Libby still expected answers fast, and at first she tried listing companies she liked. I agreed that this list of companies was part of her journey, but it wasn't the whole excursion — especially since Libby often got stalled in overanalyzing one company or comparing it with another. I said that there were bound to be companies she had never heard of, and that by only considering businesses she knew, she was restricting her vision.

I suggested that Libby attend job fairs, business conventions, and meetings in town. I told her to chart her reactions. The goal was to learn — not to make decisions. Soon Libby was able to unveil vital things about herself. She knew that her skills and areas of expertise included sales, marketing, and anything to do with homes. Another pattern emerged that surprised her — she was gravitating toward companies with offices overseas.

"For the first time I not only felt *hopeful* that I would come up with ideas, but also *optimistic*. I didn't exactly have a firm plan, but I was seeing that people were responding to me positively and that there were tons of companies and opportunities I had never even considered."

Libby's sense of optimism increased when she realized that her desire to live abroad was very strong. "I guess I've always wanted *out* of my family background. I mean *really* far out of it — like far away, in another country. Call it running away if you want. To me it was like confirming that there were lots of ways to live. Seeing how different people lived life in other countries made me feel freer, more optimistic. I didn't feel trapped anymore."

GOING FOR THE GOAL

Her Visioneering complete, Libby narrowed her search to companies with overseas offices that dealt with home products. On a whim she answered an ad for people to "create a home away from home." The ad intrigued her. It was in the *Wall Street Journal*, so she figured the company had a greater chance of being legitimate. It turned out the company was the overseas branch of a large real estate broker, builder, and development corporation. The company developed high-end resort condominiums in Florida and targeted certain

European markets where the buyers were able to afford second and sometimes third vacation properties.

"It was ideal — it was sales, it was overseas, and it had to do with homes. I didn't know Florida, but I could learn. I had been selling dream kitchens in dream homes for years. I knew what people wanted."

Libby responded to the ad, landed an interview, and was very excited. She researched the company thoroughly, even taking a long "work-vacation" to the various sites in Florida. "I was in shock. This was a great company. Their product was first-class quality all the way."

She was called back for second and third interviews, and she had her hopes up. When Libby didn't hear back from the company in a week, she was outraged. She called the vice presidents who had interviewed her and asked whether they were still interested. They said yes, but that they had reservations. They were worried that Libby would not accept a lower starting salary than she had been accustomed to. They were also concerned because she had never lived overseas.

Libby met each reservation by telling the executives how motivated she was. She explained how careful, well-thought-out, and methodical her search had been. She even offered to give them my name if they wanted any doubts cleared up. Finally, the company agreed to send Libby to Germany on a trial basis. They made no promises that she would be put in charge of that office. The initial financial arrangements were for less money than for the managerial/sales position originally advertised, but they said that if she worked out, they would promote her and increase her compensation. "It wasn't ideal — I was taking a chance — but so were they."

The company flew Libby to Florida, where she spent several weeks learning the ins and outs of the business. A few weeks later they sent her to Germany. "I loved it. There were lots of Americans, and lots of people from other parts of Europe. I had a whole new life and a whole new challenge."

Six months later Libby was promoted. She was making *more* than at her old job, and she was happy. "If I hadn't taken the time to think things out thoroughly and not just jump for the sake of choosing, I would never have found this kind of life. I learned that risk is uncomfortable, but if you can tough it out, it pays off."

Libby knew, in her own words, that she was "a control freak." It took a lot of courage for her not to jump at the first ideas she had. Living with her fears for a while paid off. Libby said she felt finally in charge of her life and very *competent*. "Who would have thought I'd be living in Germany on the banks of a river, selling dream homes?" Libby had absorbed a useful lesson about fears, anxiety, the unknown, and toughing it out.

Though impatient with the Visioneering phase, she spent enough time with it that she avoided choosing the wrong destination. She was flexible enough to extend her soul-searching until everything merged. Then she persisted when the company she wanted to work for had reservations. Thanks to the effort she'd invested in Visioneering, she was so sure of her dream that she managed to sell her new employers on it, too!

> *"Who are you?" said the caterpillar* . . . .
> *"I — I hardly know, sir, just at present — at least I know who I was when I got up this morning, but I think I must have been changed several times since then."*
> —Lewis Carroll,
> Alice in Wonderland

Are today's women inventing a mid-life crisis for their gender? Quite possibly. Elliott Jaques, a psychoanalyst, coined the term "mid-life crisis" in 1965, pessimistically defining it as the point when you stop growing up and start growing old. Perhaps a more apt description is a sense of free-floating in space with no star to guide you.

A pivotal life event may be prompting you to reevaluate: a divorce, a friend's or relative's cancer, the death of a close friend or acquaintance, a parent's death, the marriage of a child, an empty nest, children starting school, or the loss of a job. All can initiate a perfectly healthy reassessment of goals and dreams. Life doesn't stop after he dies or leaves . . . or after a cancer threat . . . or after you or he retire.

Or maybe you, like some women, have repeated nightmares that tasks are somehow not completed or that something is lost and can never quite be found. Maybe no particular significant event or dream has happened to you. Yet you have found yourself asking, *Is this all there is to life?*

This mid-life recasting by women may be intensified by several recent phenomena. One of these is the new interest in exploring the subject of death. Books, movies, all media are focusing on this frontier. With frightening rise in breast cancer rates — one in every nine women is affected, with the age group thirty-five to fifty-four hit the hardest — and females' heart disease rates rising to match those of males, women are becoming much more tuned in to their own mortality. Most humans around the age of forty begin to accept that they, too, will not be around forever. The obvious question follows naturally — as it did for Libby — Am I doing what I want with my life? How can I best utilize the rest of my time here?

> *"I don't mind dying, I just don't want to be there when it happens."*
> —WOODY ALLEN

Another influence is a development that might have been called a miracle by those who lived and died a century ago: the extension of the life span. If you are an American woman who reaches the age of fifty without a life-threatening illness, you can expect to see your ninety-second birthday. As you consider that you may be only approaching the halfway mark, and as you observe other women fulfilling their dreams, perhaps you hear a nostalgic refrain: "What am I doing the rest of my life?"

More answers to that question are possible than ever before. The women's movement is no longer a movement — it's a tidal wave. Though women are still far from the ideal of full equality, they now enjoy vast professional opportunities, innumerable sources for information and expression, and terrific mentors to emulate. Watching other women's achievements may make you wonder how much you could attain.

NO TIME LIKE THE PRESENT

If you have any nagging doubts revolving around your age, I've got news for you: Your timing for embarking on a second adulthood is perfect. Whether you recognize it or not, you are a card-carrying member of a population revolution. Although it seems unbelievable, according to the U.S. Census Bureau, the fastest-growing segment of the population consists of those over 100 years of age. Many more of us are living longer.

In France in February 1997, the oldest person on earth — a woman — celebrated her 122nd birthday. The approaching turn of the century was old hat to Jeanne Louise Calment, who cheered in the last one (the year 1900) at the age of twenty-five.

In addition, the old-fashioned advice to slow down as you age could not be more wrong. Medical research results all converge on one conclusion: Activity — mental and physical — prolongs life and enhances its quality.

According to the Bureau of Labor Statistics, more and more women are remaining in the work force longer. Among women fifty-five to sixty-four years old, 41 percent were working in 1978, but last year 47 percent were still working. According to the University of Ohio's National Longitudinal Survey, most older women are working because they have to — fewer than half of them are married, and many don't have the same pension fund investments that their male counterparts do.

Even for women in a position to retire, the concept of not working doesn't mean being idle — or even being happier. National surveys of the elderly population show that working at something meaningful — paid or unpaid — promotes well-being. For most of us, our self-esteem, personal identity, social interaction, and happiness are linked to meaningful activities. Consequently, for the remainder of the nineties and into the twenty-first century, retirement is taking on a new definition: working at what you want to do, when you want to do it — but continuing to work.

Without much reflection or planning, many new retirees first volunteer for an activity that has always interested them, then accelerate toward employment in that field — almost in spite of themselves. Later life is now about change and not about seeking security.

A primary regret both men and women report at age fifty is not having taken their education more seriously. This was true both for those who were held back in their careers because of a lack of schooling, and for those who attended the most prestigious educational institutions and achieved career success. If you feel this way, it's never too late to challenge this regret. Whether you learn computer skills, get a law degree or attend junior college, the learning experience you missed before can be reclaimed. There are courses given on the Internet, home study degrees, and distance learning networks from many universities. The possibilities for education have never been greater. Today, it's common to see women seventy and older enroll and graduate from institutions of higher learning. In 1997, seventy-five years after she dropped out of the eighth grade, Mary Fasano at age eighty-nine became the oldest person to receive a Harvard degree in the university's 361 years of educating. States like Delaware are even providing incentives for older students to go back to college by offering waivers and tuition discounts at state universities. These states see senior-citizen students, many of whom are in their eighties and nineties, as enthusiastic and more focused than their younger counterparts. Late-life achievers are all around us — if you take the time to notice.

By mid-life, Olympia Dukakis had acted in many theatrical productions — but she had never received wide national exposure. Then along came the role of the mother in *Moonstruck*. She received an Oscar for Best Supporting Actress. Olympia has performed in many movies since. She probably wouldn't dream of retiring — she's having too much fun.

To many women, retirement does not look as rosy as the cruise brochures would have them believe. For some, stopping work is not an option; others, considering their longer life expectancy, are terrified of outliving their money if they do retire. Lower wages, interrupted work histories, and lack of pension benefits leave women especially vulnerable as they age. According to the American Association of Retired Persons, widows, divorced women, and never-married women are at particular economic risk.

A group of older women at the College of Staten Island in New York are doing something about it — and it's nothing that can't be done anywhere: They are going to college. Their husbands went to college, their children have college degrees, and now it's *their* turn.

Sudden Transformations

One common scenario involves the woman who finally arrives at a career peak and commands a respectable salary. Just as she begins feeling relief and pride that she can support herself if necessary, her husband retires, and he wants her to join him in traveling and recreation. If this woman gives up her job and complies fully with his wishes, she often is transformed into a caregiver for him and/or their parents.

For women who work at home, spouse retirement can be stressful. The breadwinner is suddenly home all the time, severed from everything that defined his identity. His pattern is completely upset, and so is he. The result can be interference with her schedule and activities, including scrutiny of her household management and spending habits. Now that he is home, the two are on more equal ground; his prior habits of intimidation may be met with a different response. Regardless of who retires or how well it is planned and carried out, adjustment is necessary. For both partners, it is vital to retain the visions that support their self-esteem — and especially to continue setting new goals.

Speaking of goal-diggers — when Anna Mary Robertson Moses, known as Grandma Moses, picked up a brush, dipped it in paint and applied it to a large, empty canvas to paint the village scenes she had always loved, she was seventy-eight. She had lived her life, raised her children, even had grandchildren. Painting was only a hobby. Who would ever have guessed that art connoisseurs would recognize the merit of her primitive style? Especially "at her age"! But they did. Grandma Moses went on to be known worldwide and continued her remarkable career until she was 101 years old.

What do Olympia Dukakis, Grandma Moses, and perhaps you have in common? They raised children, even grandchildren, before finally resolving to chase after long-dormant dreams. You can too. Success doesn't have to entail winning awards or making headlines. Sometimes our most gratifying achievements are the private, unsung moments we savor alone. You don't believe it? Just ask the little red hen.

This was one of my favorite childhood stories. Remember? The little red hen asked her friends to help her plant and tend her wheat crop — only to have them, one after another, turn her down. When the wheat crop was ready, the hen finally harvested it — all by herself. She then baked the most delicious cake from the flour. When her friends smelled the cake baking, they rushed over to eat the same cake they had all refused to help make.

Yes, this is a story about selfishness and greed — but it is also a tale of a rather brave little hen who, above all, believed in her idea of baking a cake and her ability to make it happen. Most importantly, the little red hen never let her friends' lack of support stop her from envisioning her success.

The term "mid-life crisis" or "mid-life evaluation" is a misnomer because it happens to people at various ages and sometimes more than once. Often as we pass the age of fifty or sixty, another self-reflecting phase sets in. At this point we seek whatever holds the most compelling meaning and value for us; we have a strong urge to build a life characterized by integrity, from which everything else flows.

Whatever your age, it's not too late. But you have little time to lose. Begin your Visioneering now — to make the next phase of your life a consummation of your fantasies, your talents, and your life's calling.

*W*here *T*o?

Y ou always get a first chance to make a second adulthood. In
   fact, you get as many chances as you like — some people are
   on their third or fourth adulthood. But you must be committed. Of course it's easier to stay parked by the side of the road; if
you don't move, nothing bad can happen. But nothing good can
happen either.

Today's most fulfilled women realize they are responsible for their
own destiny. They appreciate that true happiness springs full-blown
from self-approval. And they know that defining their life's ambition
requires first a painful shedding of old, self-limiting beliefs about what
they should be doing — followed by a difficult search to uncover a
fresh goal or unlock a dream that has been long neglected or forgotten.

This section is about identifying your purpose for your second
adulthood — your destiny, your vision. You have reached the conclusion that change would be a good thing for you right now — but are
clueless about which direction to take. Our next task is to plot a new
course for you, one that follows your heart.

Let's get started with a personal inventory exercise, keeping an eye
toward your new and improved future:

EXERCISE 13: CHARTING YOUR DREAMS
Fill in the following vision chart as completely as you can:

I am this kind of person	who likes	who has these skills	who values
(list adjectives that best describe you)	(list all the things you like. Don't worry if they don't "fit" together in one vision)	(List your strengths and skills)	(List the principles ideals, and guiding rules that influence you)

Adapted from *Women, Work and Incest* by Dr. Lesliebeth Berger

Look at your responses. Do you see any patterns or themes? For example, one woman — Cheryl — found that she is an "outspoken" person, who tends to like "organizing people, leading meetings," and "discussing politics and social concerns." She discovered she has skills in "public speaking," "facilitating," and "motivating." She values "community action," "making a difference," and "improving social conditions." Cheryl then asked herself: *Do these discoveries about myself fit with my vision? Do they lead me to other variations of my vision?*

Cheryl was able to confirm that her desire to pursue local politics by joining a welfare-to-work committee was "right on track." In fact, she added "working with displaced homemakers" to her list. And it was a good thing she did: She couldn't get on the welfare-to-work task force but she succeeded in joining a program for displaced and battered homemakers. That was several years ago; now Cheryl is a consultant for various social service and political organizations. Had she not completed and studied her vision review chart, she might not have thought of an alternative when her first option fell through.

Explore your list. Then step back from it for a minute. What kind of person do you see? What can you picture this person doing? What else could this kind of person do? Is your vision consistent with what you see on the chart?

Focusing on yourself so intensely at this juncture may feel uncomfortable, even selfish. What others need is always easier to identify and fulfill than your own needs. While taking care of others, you manage quite nicely to avoid self-examination. Worse still, you most likely were taught and rewarded for ignoring your own wishes; women are still encouraged and admired for living a life dedicated to others instead of themselves.

Maybe you actually believe what Groucho Marx said he felt: "I wouldn't want to belong to any club that would accept me as a member."

To succeed at Visioneering, you must remember two very important rules: First, don't worry about finding what you want. Second, concentrate on what you *don't* want. I'm serious. We often know more about what we dislike than about what we enjoy. Try one of the following exercises, or do both.

Exercise 14: What Don't You Want?
Complete the following sentences: (These do not have to be job related.)

1. I dislike doing _____.
2. The things I hate most now are _____.
3. I am really fed up with the following: _____.

Let it all out. Write down everything you are fed up with, or things you just find no gratification in doing. This list serves to zoom in on what is missing from your life now.

Here's the second part of this Visioneering exercise: Hold a personal brainstorming session. Write down any ways to spend time that appeal to you. Regardless of how outlandish you might think they are, don't reject any ideas. For example, maybe you have always wanted to be a street performer or own a restaurant.

If you like where you work but find your job boring, come up with some options for changing your situation. You might request more responsibility, trade tasks with a coworker, register for a class that will enhance your chances for promotion or for a lateral switch in positions, take a do-it-yourself career change test, or seek career counseling. Roam a bookstore, browse the Web, look through an old scrapbook. Creative thinking is disorganized, directionless, random.

Here are some questions to help you calibrate your internal compass to direct you to *your* happiness:

Who are your role models? Whom do you compare yourself with? What qualities do these people have? By whose standard do you define contentment?

What three things feel like fun to you? Have these pleasures changed in the past five years? What would you like your reward to be five years from now?

What do you consider your greatest successes? What would make you feel completely fulfilled? Are you passionate about what you are doing and who you are doing it for?

How would you describe "going for it"?

Are your home life and your external life in balance?

What would you change in your life to make yourself happier?

Such questions may seem frivolous or look like a waste of time. But this is how you become you — how inventions occur to people: they put together two thoughts that were floating around unlinked. Reinvent yourself — or invent yourself for the first time.

If you are having trouble with a freeform question-and-answer approach to Visioneering, try the following exercise to help focus your aspirations.

EXERCISE 15: HERE LIES MYSELF

Ask yourself, *If I died, what would I want written as my epitaph? Who would come to my funeral and what would they say about me?*

You may find this morbid, but sometimes imagining that time has run out helps us reset our priorities. It's a little like the "Two-minute Warning" you received in Part One of this book, but this time you have the opportunity to be more reflective, and to observe yourself from a distance.

Perhaps you know people who have faced life-threatening illnesses and made revolutionary changes in their priorities as a result; usually they wish they had done it sooner. You, I hope, have the advantage of not being in a crisis; no good argument can be made for not doing what you want with your life right now. But for some, imagining a sense of urgency helps bring their vision into focus more quickly.

Other tactics can aid you in the all-important radical step of viewing your possibilities within an entirely new framework. It may help to disobey some rules your parents taught you: Talk to strangers (about what they do and why). Look for chaos, contradictions, confusion (you may see a connection among them that no one has seen before).

Explode the status quo by embracing change. Be an information junkie — search everything you hear, read, or learn for opportunities. Keep heading down your boulevard of green lights; for each one you pass, another will appear. Don't be afraid to change lanes or take an exit to check out some dazzling potential you'd never considered. Remarkably, what you're likely to come across is yet another thoroughfare with an endless row of green lights.

The kind of freewheeling excursion I'm now urging you to embark on does have a point: You need to unleash your imagination and let the ideas flow. Your best insights and breakthroughs will happen at the strangest times: when you are taking a shower, while you are driving, while you are waiting in line at the bank. It's uncanny when you are desperate to solve some problem, how when you *stop* concentrating and focusing all your energy on the task or challenge and let your thoughts drift almost playfully, the solution pops into your mind.

Creative effort requires some time, some space, and reduction of clutter. What may seem like wasted effort spent daydreaming is actually constructive time. You are letting go of the endless details of everyday life and reviving your inner spirit — which may hold long-imprisoned visions for your future.

Prisoners of war use daydreaming to survive and remain sane. During the long hours he endured in isolation as a hostage in Beirut, Terry Anderson used his imagination to create survival scenarios and plans for the future. When debriefed upon release, he said it was his ability to stay optimistic about the future that had kept him alive. Anderson didn't limit his focus only to setting goals for when he would be set free; instead he used the time to map out the steps to his goal. He held his spirits high by concentrating on what he really hoped for and then he visualized, sometimes in minute detail, how to get there — one step at a time.

> *"If you dream it, you can do it."*
> —Walt Disney

Be a Virtual Virtuoso

You've heard of virtual reality, a technology designed for computer games: The participant becomes immersed in a simulated environment displayed on a computer screen. People can find themselves extraordinarily involved in a virtual reality scenario. They groan and cheer as if everything on the screen were actually happening to them. These sophisticated interactive games are showing up everywhere from grocery stores to bars.

Now I'd like to introduce you to what I call *virtual visioning* — a mental form of virtual reality. We will use it to both Visioneer and then Visioncraft your quest. In your self-created environment, you will experience firsthand what your dream looks like, how those involved might react to your plans and goals, and how realistic the plan is.

Unfettered by risks or consequences, you will create, map, and carry out your second adulthood — without leaving the comfort of your favorite chair. In fact, you can do this anywhere. Once you get the hang of formulating your own virtual vision (using the insides of your eyelids for a projection screen), you are free to picture more leisure time, a new job, a change of lifestyle, a new family member, communing with nature. Vast possibilities like these are created effortlessly and harmlessly through this technique.

EXERCISE 16: VIRTUAL VISIONING

While most virtual reality pursuits are designed for pure enjoyment, remember that for you, this exercise also has a very important point. You will be given four scenarios to choose from, and you should pick the one that most draws you to the dreams you began to uncover in your Visionalysis. Note as you proceed whether you are following the route of nurturing or the route of achieving. Virtual visioning should set you free — but it's the freedom to move forward, not to wander aimlessly, that you're aspiring to.

Ready? Grab your imaginary goggles and let's get going. Before pulling out onto your vision superhighway, familiarize yourself with the sophisticated technology and navigation systems in your Visionmobile: Your collision-avoidance system automatically activates when you are too close to danger and signals you when the coast is clear for a lane change. Your onboard computer keeps track of your position and gives continual feedback about upcoming roadblocks so you arrive at your destination the quickest and safest way. And your vision-performance module keeps you alert so you don't miss exits or stop at any green lights.

See yourself now, pulling out onto the highway. It's okay to feel apprehensive. Remember you are in charge here, calm and relaxed. Ahead of you is a series of traffic lights as far as you can see, synchronized for a safe, smooth, and enjoyable journey. Now here's the best part: Even though all the lights you see may be red, you can turn them green. That's right, your Visionmobile has a remote control like the one for your TV that will turn any red lights green. And — wonder of wonders — you are finally and permanently in charge of this little device.

Now that you have mentally merged onto the virtual vision super-highway, choose one of the following scenarios:

1. A day at the perfect job.
2. A day of relaxing with no obligations.
3. A day that makes you feel fulfilled and content.
4. A day on vacation.

Now, start that day. Where are you? How old are you? What do you look like? What are you wearing? Are you alone? What city are you living in or near? What are you doing? How are others acting toward you? What is your opinion of yourself?

This is just a suggestion for using virtual visioning. You can use it anytime, anywhere you like, to help prioritize what has value for you and help you envision the changes you decide to make. It can also help you comprehend others' reactions to your new behavior.

Be spontaneous with your visioning, so that you surprise yourself. Stop and engage in some unplanned activity (a picnic, swinging on swings, buying a blouse at the mall — anything you want). Pay special attention to your feelings as you encounter each new setting. Experience this fun fully until it is comforting, exciting, and nurturing. When you have completed your mini-adventure and are ready to board the Visionmobile again, ask yourself the following questions:

What made what I did so pleasant? What past positive feelings were aroused by my experience? Do I ever engage in this activity now? If not, why not? How did my fantasy express one of my needs? Who was in my fantasy? Overall, what does this fantasy tell me about the difference between my current life and what I wish for? What reasons am I giving myself for not making my fantasies real?

"Imagination is more important than knowledge."

—ALBERT EINSTEIN

TRYING DREAMS ON FOR SIZE

Now is the time to let your imagination walk around a little in the real world, without taking any irrevocable steps at this point. Talking to friends is a good way to start your Visioneering. Tell them you are exploring some options for the next part of your life. Ask them what they think. Be careful, however, because friends and family often have unspoken motives: They may feel challenged by your ambition, or they may be afraid of losing you, so they might dispense discouraging advice. That doesn't bother you, because at this point you're simply absorbing new ideas. Talk to everyone: professionals, people at parties, customers in the beauty salon, neighbors walking their dogs. People love living and fantasizing vicariously; you might be amazed at what they come up with for you.

A good way to further define your ambition is to spend half an hour in front of a well-stocked magazine rack (your library or the new super bookstores have extensive selections). See what headlines interest you, what topics make you want to read the articles. The numerous little ads in the backs of magazines often have creative offerings. Don't worry about shaping your vision completely right now. The process is every-thing. The more you focus on searching, the more clearly your vision will come into view. Try to avoid concentrating on final decisions. Eventually, all the ideas you considered along the way will take shape.

Make every errand you run an expedition to explore your next adulthood. Stop by a community college and ask for a catalog. Whether or not you attend, the list of classes and major areas of study will set your creative circuitry humming. Check out an Internet bulletin board, create your own Web page, spend time in a chat room online. Look in your newspaper for discussion groups and drop by for a meeting. You have nothing to lose and everything to gain.

I must, however, add a caveat: You need to suspend your judgment at this point. When consulting others about your ambitions, beware of people who have all the answers. Learn to tune out all-knowing mentors or guides. Instead, value your own emotions, intuition, and intellectual thoughts. Don't let someone become a backseat driver on your quest.

If you set your musings free, they will assemble themselves into some orderly formation. To help you see how this works, I'll tell you the story of Teresa.

T E R E S A

Teresa was thirty-nine, never married — and in a deep panic. For several years she had been a senior analyst with a major investment firm. She was the first person in her Hispanic family of six children to attend college and have a white-collar career. Her parents were Mexican itinerant farm workers who labored hard for every nickel. Teresa promised herself early in life that she would go to college — and only have herself to take care of. "I saw how my parents struggled. Sometimes we ate nothing but potatoes. You can't imagine how many different ways you can prepare potatoes. I took a good look at their life, and I said, "not for me." It was going to be me and just me. No one else to worry about."

Teresa was rightfully proud of her accomplishments in the investment industry. She made lots of money, took expensive vacations, and went on shopping sprees whenever she wanted to. Teresa had many friends, mostly married friends with children. "I never thought I'd want kids. I saw how raising me and my brothers and sisters were problems enough for my parents. And then, boom, I don't know exactly what happened, but suddenly I realized how lonely I was, that all I had was my work, this company. I had made my so-called mark . . . but so what? That's what I was thinking — so what. I made it, I did it, it was over. I wanted not just more, but something else. Yes, that's it. I wanted something else. And then I met Rick."

Rick was a computer engineer with two teenagers from his first marriage. He and Teresa hit it off immediately. She let Rick know she wanted children of her own, and he agreed. Less than a year later they were married, and within a few months Teresa was pregnant.

After her daughter Marita was born, Teresa quit her job. "I had had enough of working. At least that's what I thought. We did not need my income, and I realized Marita was probably going to be my only chance at motherhood. I didn't want to miss a single second with her."

At first Marita brought delight to Teresa. But when she turned three, Teresa began getting depressed. "I don't know why it set in then, it just did. Maybe because Rick was traveling more, and it was just Marita and me at home watching *Sesame Street* over and over again. One day I looked at her little face and thought, 'I want her to go to college, to have a career, and to learn the importance of being able to take care of herself. At this rate, all she'll ever know is that mommies are tired, cranky, and depressed.' But the thought of going back to work made me even *more* exhausted.

"I didn't want to work full-time—I simply did not have the energy. In my field, well, it's all or nothing; there weren't any part-time jobs. They didn't exist. I thought about consulting, but running from one company to another, marketing myself, making tons of phone calls, that didn't seem the answer either. Besides, to be perfectly honest, not every company wants a Hispanic woman as a consultant."

By the time Teresa came to see me, her thoughts were swirling in chaotic circles. She was depressed, drained, and pessimistic about her life. The first thing we addressed was her *hopeless* thinking. Broad generalities are fertile soil for germinating a pessimistic outlook on life. Teresa was filled with them: consulting's no good; working full-time's no good; there's nothing part-time in my industry.

I asked Teresa to put her global negative thinking on hold until we explored as many options as possible. I suggested that she write on a piece of paper the following words: "I haven't finished conducting my search for other options. If, after I finish my search, I still can't come up with anything, then I can feel hopeless." Every time Teresa felt depressed, she read what was written on the paper. She kept it tacked up on her refrigerator and her bathroom mirror.

The next Visionalysis assignment I gave Teresa was to go to her local library and read several back issues of various finance, business, and investment magazines. I wanted her to pay special attention to profiles and biographies of up-and-coming people featured in these magazines. I told Teresa I didn't care how old the magazine was, she just had to keep reading. I asked her to report her findings to me in a few days. I deliberately shortened the time between sessions because I wanted Teresa to cram in lots of material all at once; she needed a blitz on her pessimistic thinking.

When Teresa returned to my office a few days later, she said she hadn't found any answers to her dilemma, but she had noticed that people were doing things other than consulting or being workaholics. She didn't get any ideas specifically for herself, she said, but she now felt more *hopeful* that there were other ways to work.

Teresa continued reading articles, until one day she found something that clicked: she decided she wanted to teach a business course in a university setting. She now had a plan. The next step was to contact all the local universities and business schools. Teresa set up appointments, went to interviews, and sparked some interest. She was, for the first time, beginning to feel *optimistic* because she saw her decision as *realistic* and *possible*, given her educational background, industry experience, and geographic constraints. Teresa could develop and hold onto a vision of herself as competent and positive, because she was able to see her own possibilities assume a feasible new pattern.

It took almost six months for Teresa to get a position teaching a course at a local business college, and many times she felt herself falling back on negative thinking. But then she reminded herself of her resolution to research all the possibilities before feeling hopeless. Whenever Teresa became discouraged she recalled these indisputable facts: Colleges in her geographic area — and their needs — change from semester to semester. In the end, the job she did get was filling in for a woman on maternity leave.

After Teresa taught her first course, she felt vital — without having to sacrifice much time away from her daughter Marita. When the semester — along with her job — ended, Teresa lapsed into being a little pessimistic again; I reminded her that she now had at least three things she didn't have before: experience teaching, contacts, and, most important, the stirrings of a sense of mastery.

Teresa called back all the schools she had previously approached, making sure to mention the names of the professors and department heads she had met at the business school. Wisely, she stayed in touch with these people; she secured complimentary references from her colleagues and supervisor. Within three months Teresa was offered the chance to teach two courses in the business school of the city community college.

No pivotal life event prompted Teresa to reevaluate. But when she became depressed she saw only red lights and was even stopping at green ones. Once she realized she could make turns and explore — that there was more than one route to her destination — her accelerator became unstuck and off she went.

> *"If we all did the things we are capable of doing, we would literally astound ourselves."*
> —THOMAS EDISON

No Buts About It

Perhaps your mind keeps stalling on the thought, *It's all well and good to daydream, but it will never happen to me.* You are absolutely right: it won't happen *to you;* you must make it happen. The word BUT promotes self-limiting beliefs we handily use as excuses to defend not pursuing our visions. Here are some of the most common YES-BUT:

YES I want to travel the country in an RV, BUT what if I get sick?

YES I would like to go back to work, BUT my family will be mad.

YES I would like to learn to draw, BUT everyone will laugh at me.

YES I would like to exercise regularly, BUT I don't like the idea of working out where others can see my body.

Beliefs are like getting stuck in a ditch — the more you spin your wheels, the more stuck you stay. That's why it is so necessary, at this point in your Visioneering, to get off your BUT.

You have no way of knowing initially what it will take to make your plan succeed, so you can't say with any absolute assurance that it will fail. Your strategy will change as you pursue your goal; if your life has been neat, orderly, predictable, you'll need to let in some uncertainty. Remember Edison's three thousand attempts to invent the light bulb: We now enjoy light after sunset, because he was willing to reinvent the path toward his ultimate vision. Edison's was certainly *not* a straight or narrow route that was easy to follow. Your successful plan may look like his — full of combinations, deletions, and fragments of failed attempts.

I know it's hard to balance your vision search while having other priorities and responsibilities to juggle. It's difficult to read the map, watch the road signs, and look for green lights amid the crowded byways of your everyday life. But you must remain focused, ensuring your self-expression nourishes you and others simultaneously. Make sure you give voice to your innermost self. Keep your eyes on the road.

Remember the popular movie *Field of Dreams?* Kevin Costner plays the role of a midwestern farmer who hears a voice telling him, "If you build it, they will come." In answer to this call, he builds a baseball diamond in the middle of his cornfields. The ghosts of baseball legends emerge from the corn rows and begin to play.

This ordinary farmer acted on a passion, a vision. He lived his fantasy — despite criticism. He listened to his inner voice. You can, too.

And he worked with what he had. You must also. Take a closer look at what is within reason and what isn't. For example, what if, at forty-five years of age, you have a vision of having a child with your new husband, but he has children from a previous marriage and has undergone a vasectomy. Is it realistic to thinkl that his procedure can be reversed? Maybe adoption or fertilization by a donor are more viable options.

Or maybe you want desperately to move out of a cold climate, but the place you have chosen does not have good job opportunities or affordable housing. When you first envision your dream, it is likely to seem unrealistic. When you test it out, however, you find it can be accomplished — perhaps with a few alterations. At other times, like the farmer in *Field of Dreams,* you have to go for it — take the risk and do it anyway, even if you think your chances for success are slim.

EXERCISE17: YOU OUGHTA BE IN PICTURES
Now it's time to make your own movie. Pick a few of your favorite quests and improvise a script for their successful completion. The show you are about to see is the rest of your life — your second adulthood (or maybe your third or fourth). It's a feature-length preview of coming attractions.

But this time, you're not the supporting actress, speaking your lines under the instruction of a director. You'll need to redefine how you relate to the other players in the cast and also the stage crew. Picture yourself differently: You're the star, the screenwriter, the director, and the producer.

As glamorous as it sounds, this role adaptation can be difficult. You may be accustomed to thinking of yourself as untalented, uninspired, a workaholic, not an interesting person. Come on, stretch your imagination and get into your character. Feel more comfortable in a new, healthier self-identity.

Now let's try a variation of this process: Reflect on your childhood, and make a movie of your own real-life memories.

When we are young, we are endlessly curious and open-minded — exactly the traits needed to bring about change in our adult selves. Think back now to how you played as a child. What games did you favor? How did you use your imagination to cope with pain or fear? What did you do every day after school, in the summer, on Saturdays? Who was that child who wrote silly poems or drew pictures with chalk on the sidewalk? What excited you then? Adult creativity requires reawakening the spontaneous child within, the willingness to consider all options, to try all possibilities. You need to recapture the adventure of doing something with no purpose in mind. Such fantasies and imaginary journeys are true reflections of your real self. If you smother the flames of your dreams and passions, you will put out the fire of fulfillment. It's possible to be too serious, too responsible, too confined by others' definitions of success or happiness.

In this chapter you've learned to let your imagination take the wheel for a while and go for a spin along delicious possibilities without any fear of collisions. You saw how Teresa let her thoughts wander free, conducting research to urge them along, until they took her where she wanted to go. Next, we'll put you back in the driver's seat. Your Visioneering has produced some notions of where you might venture; now we need to make sure that you're ready to make the trip.

chapter 7

*Y*ou're the *D*river

At this point, you may be saying to yourself, *What was I thinking of? I have no skills to pursue any goal — much less one I shelved long ago.* You're stopping at a green light, aren't you? Let's get you past these nagging doubts by pressing on with your Visioneering. Make a list of tasks you do every week (schedule an entire family's transportation for example), every month (balance the checkbook and handle accounts payable and receivable), every year (prepare tax return or collect information for a tax professional). List your achievements — big and small. A great way to demonstrate your own worth to yourself is to acknowledge tasks you took responsibility for and completed. Include anything you are proud to have done.

Look back through your calendar or your personal journal to remind yourself of these accomplishments. You might even peruse old calendars. Write out a job description for what you are doing now. Ask yourself: *Did I develop something? Did I initiate something* (in the family, neighborhood, community)? *Did I improve something* (landscaping, replacing tile in a bathroom, redecorating a bedroom, purchasing items your household needed)? *Did I complete a project within budget? Did I prepare any original documents* (bylaws, manuals, guidelines)? Remember, nothing is unimportant.

If you have not been employed for some time, or have not been in school recently, the word "skills" may seem intimidating. When we traditionally think of skills only in terms of employment and education, we ignore the other source for skill improvement: experience. Skills are defined as expertise that comes from training *or experience;* they may or may not be job-related. Your vision may not involve a job. Look over the following list and check off those skills you can claim. They're the same words you'll see on any resume. You'll be surprised by how many of these skills you already possess:

Numerical and Organizational Skills

____ Financial bookkeeping

____ Managing budgets (household, recreational)

____ Allocating resources (paying bills)

____ Cost analysis (car purchases)

____ Keeping deadlines

____ Organizing/classifying/filing/processing records

____ Making arrangements/contacts

____ Paying attention to details

____ Making decisions

____ Implementing decisions

Problem Solving Skills

____ Gathering information

____ Clarifying problems

____ Organizing/classifying research materials

____ Diagnosing/finding the root of the problem

____ Troubleshooting

____ Anticipating problems

____ Analyzing/dissecting/subdividing challenges

____ Testing solutions

____ Reviewing/critiquing/evaluating solutions

Observational and Analytical Skills

____ Sensing, feeling, listening

___ Perceiving potential in others
___ Assessing/appraising
___ Observing/reflecting
___ Reasoning/abstracting/applying logic

Human Relation Skills
___ Caring for others/empathizing
___ Counseling/guiding
___ Collaborating with others
___ Advocating/negotiating for others
___ Acting as host
___ Being sensitive; listening and understanding
___ Communicating warmth
___ Participating in teamwork
___ Motivating others
___ Creating pleasant environments

Management Skills
___ Organizing and coordinating others
___ Establishing procedures
___ Reviewing/evaluating
___ Hiring/team-building
___ Developing people's potential
___ Delegating responsibility
___ Managing responsibility
___ Designing and developing programs
___ Supervising others
___ Planning/forecasting

Communications/Public Relation Skills
___ Writing reports/memos

____   Translating information/explaining
____   Writing promotional materials
____   Using humor
____   Telling stories
____   Editing and reading
____   Defining and summarizing
____   Public speaking
____   Demonstrating
____   Making radio and TV presentations
____   Performing in public

Instructional Educational Skills
____   Briefing/explaining/advising/informing
____   Leading/facilitating
____   Encouraging/enabling others to help themselves
____   Teaching/mentoring/tutoring/training
____   Creating learning environments
____   Illustrating concepts
____   Using examples

Leadership Skills
____   Initiating/self-directing
____   Managing time efficiently
____   Persisting
____   Confronting problems head on
____   Planning and promoting change
____   Proactively solving problems
____   Taking risks
____   Making complex decisions
____   Setting an example for others
____   Motivating others

___ Inspiring others
___ Chairing meetings
___ Persuading others
___ Influencing others
___ Selling/negotiating/bargaining
___ Promoting ideas
___ Reconciling conflicts
___ Mediating

Physical and Mechanical Skills

___ Coordinating plant care: gardens, landscaping
___ Farming/animal care
___ Traveling/navigating
___ Outdoor work/wilderness leadership
___ Athletic endeavor
___ Cleaning/tending/cooking
___ Art/crafts/dancing
___ Technical/mechanical reasoning (invention, construction)
___ Spatial perception (choreography)
___ Designing, shaping, composing (graphic art)
___ Operating equipment/using tools
___ Repairing/assembling/installing
___ Building/construction

Creative/Imaginative/Innovative Skills

___ Imagining/intuiting
___ Improvising/inventing
___ Innovating/creating ideas
___ Experimenting/developing/formulating
___ Synthesizing/integrating
___ Predicting/showing foresight

___ Adapting/improving/showing insight
___ Designing new programs
___ Sensing/appreciating/evaluating beauty
___ Expressing verbally or nonverbally
___ Creating music/art/photography/sculpture
___ Visualizing shapes/colors/concepts
___ Symbolizing words/images/concepts
___ Writing poems/plays/stories
___ Acting/staging/directing productions

As you ran through this checklist, did you notice anything about the items you picked or how they relate to each other? Do your choices fit something you'd like to pursue?

Perhaps your dream of traveling the world in a sailboat is beyond the reach of your abilities, your time and your finances. You need to be sensible if you're going to fit your "lost opportunity" into your current life with its responsibilities.

A DOSE OF REALITY

Visioneering requires weighing the pluses and minuses of the outcomes you're considering. Ask yourself the following questions: *What will I gain or lose by my choice? How will I feel about myself afterwards? Will those closest to me gain or lose from my decision?* This way you get to taste-test what may appear to be appetizing options.

Hang onto the thoughts and emotions you've been gathering, as we zoom in on your current priorities and reservations about change.

EXERCISE 18: MUST-HAVES

Even if your vision is clear at this point, I recommend that you write in your notebook a list of MUST-HAVES. These are bottom-line requirements that you consider necessary in any decision you make. For example, you wish to get a part-time job, but you want to be home when your children arrive from school. If you are considering having your parents come to live with you, a must-have might be hiring a cleaning person two times a week. Or if you yearn to go to law school, the must-have could be a commitment from your husband to cook for himself.

Other possible must-haves are listed below. Check any that apply to you; but more important, add your own items to the list:

___ Ability to travel

___ A flexible work schedule

___ No snow or ice

___ Enough snow to ski

___ My children nearby

___ Meaningful challenge

___ Fun

___ Lots of time for leisure activities

___ Challenging job

___ Domestic help

___ Opportunities to socialize

___ More time with my partner

___ At least $X income

___ Control of my life

___ Simpler lifestyle

___ Less stress

___ Safe, enjoyable place to exercise outdoors

___ A first, second child

___ My grandchildren nearby

___ Fewer responsibilities

___ More time for home life

Now rank your must-haves in order of their importance to you. Securing your must-haves and accomplishing your mission at the same time would be terrific, but it is not always possible. You'll be better at selecting what to compromise on after you have ranked your must-haves. You're learning to listen to yourself and rely on your intuition;

you're cultivating the ability to follow your inner spirit just to see where it leads. Stay with the process, and trust it; it's working for you!

> *"Opportunities are usually disguised as hard work, so most people don't recognize them."*
> —ANN LANDERS

FEELING YOUR WAY

Women's intuition or gut feelings have often been maligned as silly and unimportant. It is critical that you listen to yours, because your subconscious emotions can tip the scale of decision in one direction or the other. In a 1996 study by the National Foundation of Women Business Owners, more than 53 percent of the working women surveyed emphasized intuitive thinking; they stress sensitivity and creativity as valuable qualities in their jobs. They viewed their businesses as families and networks, and believed they were better than men at balancing personal and professional priorities.

People often describe the intuitive portion of their decision-making as "soul-searching," "mulling it over," "following the heart," "looking inside oneself," "praying," or — perhaps the most popular — "sleeping on it." You need to pay close attention when something "feels right." Your body's cruise control system is telling you: *Don't stop at this green light.* Honor your perceptions and a priori reasoning as part of a balanced set of information you use when making a decision. Never underestimate your hunches.

This doesn't mean you abandon the critical thinking you learned to apply during your Visionalysis. Analyzing your instincts and delving into their origin is also important, because you may be drawn to a particular profession or possible vision simply because it is familiar. Perhaps your mother or father or uncle or former teacher would approve of it. These may not be useful instincts; they are not purely derived from you and the person you want to become.

Not all your fondest desires will reveal themselves at once; your intuition doesn't work that way. You must pay careful attention during this critical time. When you come across something that moves you, make a mental note of it — better yet, write it in your journal.

Don't be surprised to find that what excites you makes you anxious at the same time. A well-kept secret of fulfilled people is that they often feel uneasy while chasing their dreams. But they channel their tension so that it works for them. Besides, a little apprehension can be fun: Think of the last time you walked into a party, a noisy room packed full of people. Even though you knew everyone and were delighted to be there, it was both exhilarating and perhaps a little scary for a few seconds. But at the end of the evening, you described it as fun — a great party.

As you drive closer to your aspirations, you'll stir up a lot of emotions, both pleasurable and scary. Don't let them put the brakes on your quest. Look at the different ways people react to the same situation: I find the Tower of Terror at Disney World thrilling, while you may find it terrifying. As you search for your destiny, don't rule out things that make you feel uncomfortable, or maybe even bring you close to tears. These emotions may be the highway sign you've been looking for — with your destination written on it.

> *"Cherish your visions and your dreams as they are the children of your soul; the blueprint of your ultimate achievements."*
>
> —NAPOLEON HILL

S H A R O N

Sharon, forty-five, came from a working-class family. She graduated from high school and immediately went to work in a women's clothing boutique in her hometown. She married at twenty-two, had three boys, got divorced, was remarried, and was divorced a second time. Always, in the back of her mind, Sharon dreamed of financial independence. How could she attain it? She knew women's clothing. In fact, she had worked her way up to managing the store, but Sharon never had the resources or opportunity to own a store.

Finally, that chance came. The owner of the store Sharon was managing decided to retire. As the proprietor advertised and showed the store to potential buyers, Sharon became agitated. She began a Visionalysis to ferret out the source of her discontent. It didn't take long. She kept saying to herself, *If only I had the money, I could buy this store.* Finally, after Visioneering for a while, Sharon mustered up her courage, and approached her boss.

Through some careful mental planning, Sharon played out how she would negotiate to buy the store. She was able to borrow money from the Small Business Administration. When she took possession, she implemented all the improvements she had always envisioned for the boutique. Within three years, she was financially independent.

As with many goals we achieve, however, Sharon learned that she was not yet fully satisfied — even though she had reached her monetary target. She finally realized that financial independence was not the final link to her contentment. Because she had been convinced that her agitation came from a desire to own the store, Sharon had not practiced the Visioneering necessary to define her quest thoroughly. What she thought was her lifelong dream did not turn out to be her passion.

That wasn't the end of Sharon's story, nor was it her last reinvention of herself. When she went back to undertake Visioneering again, she recalled childhood visits to the mountains where her Grandmother had a summer home. Sharon unearthed a longing to do what she loved most — gardening.

Sharon's kids were grown; she had nothing holding her back. So she made the decision to sell the clothing store and move. She now lives in the Adirondack Mountains of upstate New York, where she opened a small garden shop. Her Visioneering transformed her from an unhappy successful entrepreneur to a fulfilled small-town shop owner. Sharon realized her second (or perhaps third) adulthood vision.

As Sharon learned, it's essential to invest time in the Visioneering stage. Remember, you're looking for subtle and evasive dreams that have been hiding for years from your conscious self. And don't overlook the possibility that you're also searching for a spiritual connection. Whatever your formal spiritual system may be, believing you are connected to a meaningful pursuit helps dissolve the doubts about whether you are traveling down the *right* road. Reaching to believe in something greater than we are is nothing new. As you age, it's natural and healthy to assess why you exist here and now.

LEAD, KINDLY LIGHT

Vocation is the word that best describes this process of spiritual discovery. Though commonly used to refer to someone's profession or occupation, vocation's first definition is "a call, summons, or impulsion to perform a certain function." Deciding where that call is coming from is up to you.

People who discover and pursue their vocation are lit up like a July Fourth fireworks display. They talk about their life's "work," with the color and exuberance of the best storytellers. They electrify the atmosphere that surrounds them; they're fun to be around.

As you pursue your second adulthood, keep your eye out for the glimmer of a calling or vocation. It's an exercise in sorting: understanding your strengths and weaknesses, questioning who you were, who you are now, and where you want to go. Bringing your vision into focus requires noticing change, identifying voids and needs in yourself. Your direction is not going to find you; you have to venture out and find it yourself.

Life's purpose becomes clearer when you have been out driving around by yourself for a while. You'll begin to gain better control and confidence, which leads to self-reliance. But fear of red lights is an essential part of that journey. When you come out of the tunnel and into the daylight, you'll feel downright invincible. Remember, Candace (back in Chapter Four) discovered her vision in her early fifties and has been pursuing it with vigor ever since.

> *"Our aspirations are our possibilities."*
> —ROBERT BROWNING

When you become an adept Visioneer, you too will be lifted to new levels of hope, perhaps even becoming giddy with the prospect that change can happen. The force released by even the possibility is powerful. I must remind you, however, that any transition takes vigilant awareness, patience, and resolve to undo familiar, ingrained ways of thinking and acting. This is not to say that the task has to be overwhelming; it can be approached like any other objective, by breaking it down into manageable bits and taking small steps one at a time.

Internal growth can be the most gratifying part of the achievement; the process — sometimes even more than the triumphs — can surprise you with its rewards. To paraphrase a former General Electric motto: Your process can be your most important product.

EXERCISE 19: THE DOTTED LINE
In exploring a prospective vision, you need to find what moves you, what you want to delve further into. That takes resolve on your part. To ensure your commitment, fill in this personal contract with yourself:

I,_____, am making this contract to take the following action:_____

_____. (Define it as best you can for the time being.)

I am going to do this much _____

_____. (Break it down into bite-sized chunks.)

I am going to do it by _____ (date). (Don't be unrealistic.)

I will continue to pursue my goal every _____ (day, week, month).

I will ask _____ to be my support person. (Pick people you trust.)

If I achieve my goal, my reward will be _____. (Be really good to yourself.)

Date: _____ Signature _____

Once you've committed your idea to paper, can you see the journey taking shape?

> *"Every organism has one and only one central need in life: to fulfill its own potentialities."*
> —ROLLO MAY

Now let's map out a route to take you where you want to go, keeping in mind that you may modify your plan — or even your final destination — as more red lights turn green for you throughout your journey.

SUMMARY: VISIONEERING

1. Today's women are living longer, working harder, and experimenting more. The sooner you give yourself permission to do the same, the more likely you are to catch up with the front of the pack.
2. Retirement is no longer a letting go of work and stimulation — if it ever was for women. If you are nearing retirement age, or worry about where retirement will take you down the road, Visioneering is essential.
3. Begin Visioneering by defining your likes and dislikes, your interests and abilities. No subject is out of bounds; set yourself free to wander and dream.
4. Gather as much information as you can, even the opinions of others, which you can allow yourself to discard later if they don't fit with your vision.
5. Don't let your YES-BUTS divert you from your course. Use virtual visioning and movie making to try on your fantasies for size.
6. To determine whether your vision is realistic, concentrate on the many abilities and experiences you already possess.
7. Use your list of MUST-HAVES to determine what your vision can't possibly do without. Where can you compromise to make it work?
8. Learn to trust your intuition and emotions, using the tools you got from Visionalysis to understand and evaluate their messages.
9. Think of your new life as a vocation or calling that will require commitment and dedication on your part. Promise yourself that you'll take that call!

part

*V*ISIONCRAFTING

chapter 8

*T*est-Driving *Y*our *D*ream

SOOK

Sook came to the United States from Korea when she was seventeen. Her parents and older brother had died of a virus that had devastated their small Korean village, and she found a home with family members already living in California. These aunts and uncles were her only relatives; her grandparents had also died years before. She began working immediately to earn her naturalized citizenship, learning quickly to adopt the ways of American teenagers.

Sook attended a large university in the Northeast, majoring in engineering. "I always felt I had to look out for myself. I had a career only because I had to, actually." Sook described herself as a farm girl who was out of place in the big city, "but what choice was there?"

After graduating from college, Sook was hired by a firm that did research for the space program. As soon as Sook had accrued enough vacation time and money, she returned to her Korean village. What she found there was not what she had expected during all her years of studying in America and longing for home.

"I was shocked. Everyone knew my name and my family, but I did not know anyone. I looked around and saw the difficult life they led. I knew if I did not leave right away, I would stay forever."

That trip "home" haunted Sook for years. "I watched every special about the Korean War, Vietnam, orphans being rescued. If a program featured anything about Cambodia, Vietnam, Korea, any of those places, I would be glued to it. When VCRs were invented, well, I was in really big trouble: One travel show on visiting Vietnam, I must have watched ten times."

Sook felt that her first duty was to her career — that she owed this to the memory of her parents, who had suffered from the loss of her brother. "My brother had died first of an infection brought on by a virus — we never really knew what kind. These viruses would sweep into our villages, kill so many, but no one ever knew why or what it was. My parents were devastated by his death.

"It didn't matter that none of them were still alive. They were alive to me . . . inside my feelings, my heart, my whole life. And of course all my aunts and uncles reminded me how proud my parents would have been to see their little Sook graduate from this big university and get this important job.

"I liked working, but more because I liked knowing I was doing a good job for a good cause. I can't say the challenges or ideas or even the work environment was particularly great. But I did not see I had any choice."

Every weekend Sook attended a Sunday afternoon meal with her aunts and uncles. They questioned Sook about her work and wanted to know what she was inventing. "Their standards for my career were very high. And I was never to complain about work."

When they weren't asking about her work, they were quizzing Sook about her social life. There were many men at work, but Sook was always shy around them. One day she met Paul, a Chinese-American engineer, and they slowly became friends through work. "We knew each other for six months before I even asked him his last name. He worked in another department, and only came down to my floor on his way to get cigarettes at the machine. He said I made him smoke more."

Paul was born in the United States, but both his parents were from China. He was an only child, and therefore was expected to achieve. He rose rapidly in the company, receiving a promotion and a substantial salary increase for skillfully refining a satellite tracking system. As soon as he received his first larger paycheck, he asked Sook to marry him. Shortly afterward, they married and moved to the Washington, D.C. area, where Paul was offered an even better job.

"We hardly knew each other. I don't think we really ever dated." Soon Sook became pregnant. "That was wonderful for us. All I had ever wanted was to raise a family." Sook gave birth to twin boys. Two years later she had another child, a daughter. "At first I did not work. I wanted to stay home with the children. That made me happy. One day, when she was three, my daughter had seizures, and she became mildly retarded. She needed constant monitoring. It was a great deal of work, but I knew that staying home and attending to her was the right thing to do."

For the remainder of her children's upbringing, until they all graduated from high school, Sook remained at home. "I was tired, but happy with my children. I was not so happy with Paul."

Sook had assumed that because of Paul's Chinese background, he would understand her Korean heritage, values, and inner conflicts. "In my culture, you didn't talk much about your feelings. There was great shame in admitting weakness or sadness. You were supposed to plod along. So I guess that's what I did. Paul — he did what he pleased, which was work, work, work." Paul saw the household duties as Sook's domain. Because he was focused on his success as an engineer, he expected her to handle the housework and the demands of their daughter's condition without any emotional or practical support from him.

Sook told no one about being unhappy in her marriage. She took pride when her twin boys excelled in school; they were attending different universities in the same city. In fact, one of the universities was Sook's alma mater, which doubly pleased her. Coincidentally, both her sons were majoring in computer science. They were not only intellectually accomplished, but also talented in sports. One son was a champion diver, and the other a champion swimmer.

Then tragedy struck. While they were driving through a storm back to college after a Thanksgiving break, the boys' car veered off the road. Both her sons were killed. Sook was devastated.

Despite her many experiences with death, adjustment to this loss tested Sook to the limit and put tremendous strain on the marriage. A year and a half after the tragedy, Sook decided to divorce Paul. She and her daughter went to live with an aging aunt. "I was depressed, relieved, and ashamed at the same time. I felt I had brought on these bad times. But how? What had I done?"

ON HER OWN

Sook received a divorce settlement, and she still would not work full-time. "I knew I could leave my daughter An with my aunt, but the truth was they both needed help and attention, so I didn't want to work any more than part-time." She found a part-time job at an engineering firm. The months following were difficult. Sook didn't even tell her aunt she was divorced; she said Paul had landed a very good job consulting and had to travel a great deal. She told the aunt that she had been lonely in their big house. The aunt tactfully asked no questions.

Then one day at work, Sook met Tom, an executive who worked at the firm. "He liked my work and he liked me. I could tell."

Some mornings they met for coffee and conversation, and Sook learned that she and Tom had a great deal in common. He had been raised by foster parents, and had been married and divorced. He didn't have any children from the marriage, and still wanted very much to start a family. But Tom was almost fifty, and growing anxious because he felt his time for having children was running out. He had never remarried, and had filled his life with work, fishing and boating, and active church membership. He was a deeply religious family man — without a family.

Sook told me she felt comfortable with Tom. "He even got along with An and my aunt. I was happy, and afraid to admit it. This sounds silly, but when he wanted to become more intimate, I said no, no, no, and no. I still believed somewhere in the back of my mind that knowing one man was enough. Inside, that little farm girl was still alive."

Tom had dated a few other women from his church and office; he was determined to remarry and have children. When he realized how old Sook and An were, he began having doubts about their relationship. He had thought both women were much younger, and he had begun to hope that Sook was the woman who would bear the children he wanted so desperately. Adjusting to the reality that Sook was close to his own age, with a grown daughter, was difficult for him. Sook knew she'd been wrong to let Tom believe she was younger, but she hadn't realized how important fatherhood was to him.

"It's easy to mistake my daughter An for a child. She is tiny, like I am, and partly because of her developmental challenges, she has the innocence of a child. As for me, I suppose this sounds old-fashioned, but I never told Tom how old I was until well into the relationship. My aunt said nothing about all this. But she knew in her own quiet way what was happening."

One day An announced she wanted to move to a group home with other developmentally challenged young adults. After investigating various facilities, Sook agreed. A week later — about ten months into the relationship — Tom decided to stop dating Sook. She was crushed. "Suddenly, I had no one. I was alone except for my aunt."

Relieved of some responsibility for her daughter, Sook returned to work full-time at the firm where she was previously employed "just to keep my mind off my troubles and combat the loneliness." But she was getting more and more depressed. It was difficult for her to feel satisfied without what she called "connection." She wanted more than anything to recreate the family life she had never had.

"I felt cheated in my marriage because Paul was never there for me. Children and a husband do not make a family. Feelings and doing things together, and loving and caring for each other — that is what makes a family. I felt I had no one but my elderly relatives and a few cousins. Most of them had moved away. I did have two cousins nearby in Maryland, but they were always busy. No one stopped over on Sundays — just holidays, that kind of thing."

It Takes a Village

By the time Sook came to see me, she was quite depressed. She felt unfulfilled, had grown to hate working, but also disliked always staying home with her elderly aunt. She saw no way out of her situation. She felt her life was over. She was in the *hopeless* stage: she blamed herself for her circumstances, and could see no other options. Her vision of the rest of her life was one of darkness, quiet, and loneliness.

After going over this long, sad story, we embarked on Sook's Visionalysis. I asked Sook, "What ideally would you like to happen in your life — even if it's impossible? What do you need to relieve your gloomy feelings?" Sook not only needed a vision of her future, she also had to identify her current needs.

Later Sook admitted, "That was hard. I didn't know I had needs — and if I did, I didn't know it was okay to have them." As part of her initial Visionalysis, Sook wrote out all the things she disliked doing in her current situation. Her list included being alone, having no one to guide her, having no one who valued her, having to go to a job and just sit and work and not feel rewarded. It was very difficult for Sook to "let it all out." She repeatedly apologized for doing what she viewed as complaining; she saw articulating her needs as demonstrating a lack of appreciation for what she had. She struggled to come up with a list of things she hated or wanted. We spent many sessions nurturing and legitimizing the expression of Sook's needs in life. Like many women, she couldn't easily give herself permission to be happy;

it was a struggle for her to focus first on what *she* needed before meeting the needs of everyone else.

Just by learning to express her needs and to believe this process was good for her, Sook gradually began to enter a more *hopeful* stage. She had acted as her own worst enemy by putting restrictions on her right to have wants. Once she gathered enough strength to fight her internal messages of self-denial, she was able to clarify what she wanted.

Finally, one day in my office, I told Sook we were ready to begin Visioneering. Sook hadn't been able to embark on this exercise until she felt more freed up to let her wishes, fantasies, and desires have full declaration.

In Visioneering there is *no self-censoring*. Sook wrote down everything she could think of that she liked. She listed things like working with others, teaching others, being part of an organization, understanding people's needs, analyzing problems. She also said she liked to work independently, didn't like schedules and deadlines, and liked surprises. The analytical part of Sook — her engineering side, she called it — liked finding solutions.

She then closely examined her list and was amazed at the pattern. "I guess I'm one of those rare engineers who like people. In fact, I think I became an engineer simply because I could. Not because I chose it."

I asked Sook what she might have chosen if she had had the chance. "Oh, well, it's too late now," she protested. She was reluctant to list other choices for fear that if she faced them, she would feel an unbearable sense of loss. It was painful for her to delve too deeply into her past and her childhood dreams.

I encouraged Sook to become a little braver. On her "engineer side," she mentioned that she would have liked to be a consultant — make her own hours and troubleshoot. On her "people side" she said, without hesitation, that she wanted a "village."

Sook was embarrassed by what had popped out of her mouth. But I knew she had revealed important information about herself, and we needed to explore it further. When I asked her what she meant by a "village," she said, "I don't know what I mean by a village." She was stumped. So I asked her to talk about her life in Korea. She sat up in surprise, "Oh my! It's so obvious. How stupid of me. I want to do something that brings people together."

We were both elated to have made some progress, but her enthusiasm was short-lived. The concept was no sooner out of Sook's mouth than she began belittling her fledgling idea. She became trapped in the YES-BUT cycle:

"Yes, but I don't know what that means."

"Yes, but how would I do it?"

"Yes, but it's a crazy idea."

"Yes, but . . ."

FINALLY GETTING SOMEWHERE

At times Sook felt overwhelmed and confused, at times hopeless and frightened. I encouraged her not to give up: We were moving into the all-important phase of Visioncrafting.

This is probably one of the easiest points in the journey at which to find an excuse to quit — the answers seem so far away and scary. And the senses of revelation and self-knowledge that come with having successfully completed Visionalysis and Visioneering can be so satisfying — and exhausting — that many people are tempted to say, "Okay, enough." It's difficult to summon up energy and enthusiasm for the remainder of the trip. Like many people, Sook found the fear of following through on her discoveries greater (in the beginning at least) than the desire to change. But Sook was determined, despite her fears, to find meaning in her life. She persisted.

Then an idea hit — what she wanted most was to establish one of those supervised homes for young adults, like the one where her daughter lived. She understood what mild retardation was like, she knew the demands of these people, and she also knew what kind of supervision they needed. For the first time since she could remember, Sook felt *optimistic*— she had an idea, she knew it was a valuable and needed service, and knew she had the preliminary skills to start it.

Sook's next step was to start the mechanics of Visioncrafting — to research how these adult care facilities make money. Who funds them? Is it lucrative? Do private sector businesses operate them? How do you get federal, state, and local funding and licensing? She had tons of questions, lots of problems to solve — one of her favorite activities. This was exactly the kind of project she loved.

In the next month Sook worked hard at investigating supervised adult homes. She began to make lots of community contacts. Eventually, she devised several plans for implementing her program. She learned that there were many different ways to establish a facility, provide quality care, and make money as well. She was feeling empowered and passionately excited. Exactly at this time, Tom called and said he had made a mistake. He couldn't forget her, he said. He had even rethought his own "life plan" and realized that, at his age, he was uncertain about whether to bring a newborn into the world. He had spoken to his pastor, who encouraged him to think of *other* ways to have a family.

The pastor's advice was excellent — he was cautioning Tom against getting stuck in *one* script, only *one* plan for the remainder of his life. "Be flexible," the pastor had advised; "something will come up."

Even though Sook had gone on with her life, she was overjoyed when Tom called. As soon as Sook and Tom got together, they discussed her new plans. He was amazed to find that they might be on the same wavelength. They resumed their relationship, and Tom put Sook in touch with the chief executive officer of their company, who had been researching greater involvement in the community. Tom hoped the executive would be helpful in raising money and contacting business and community leaders to help Sook.

As she began mapping out the detailed plan of her facility, she was alarmed to experience something else — a negative feeling. "I didn't know what it was. I felt trapped. I guess I found out setting up this kind of business was more complicated and administrative than I thought. Lots of interviewing of prospective employees, lots of paperwork. I was getting discouraged again and couldn't understand why. I had to reassess my personal goals, and I finally discovered deep in my heart that what I wanted most was not to run a facility as a business, but to take in kids myself and care for them. That was all I wanted."

When Sook expressed her confusion, Tom suggested she talk with his pastor. The pastor told her the same things Sook and I had been working on: *All* information you learn about yourself is helpful. Sook's vision was still coming into focus. "So, maybe I didn't need to feel so down. I learned to keep lots of pathways open."

SHARING THE VISION

As Sook told Tom what she was learning about herself, he became more excited. By now he knew how much he loved her; being with her was more important than sticking to his own rigid script of having a family. They both became more flexible, helping each other to become more realistic. Although Sook had begun to Visioncraft, she remained flexible enough to return to Visioneering when her research into establishing the adult home provoked less than positive feelings. Sook said that even though she didn't have anything in place, she was feeling more of a sense of mastery. She felt in charge of her dream — both the realistic and unrealistic parts; she felt more adaptable and not so stuck on one outcome. Sook now had the capability to discover things about herself and accept them.

Tom said to her one night, "Perhaps we can do this together . . . or perhaps our own version of it." Sook realized in that moment that she had discovered someone who shared her values and vision. Not too long after that, Tom gave her an engagement ring and asked her to marry him. When she accepted, Tom asked how she felt about adopting kids in need. They were considered too old to adopt nonchallenged children, but the rules for special adoption were more generous.

Tom and Sook were married and immediately started the adoption process. They started with two children with special needs. Sook said she had never felt happier. "I like this much better. I have my own private village. This suits me more than establishing a facility.

"But the important things are, I discovered what I wanted and developed a plan that allowed me to take several different routes to my goal — not just one way. And I did it all *before* Tom came back into my life. I think it was the only way to go on this: I needed to feel that my own life *by myself* was possible — that I wasn't just hooking onto someone else's dream. I felt really *in charge* of my own life; Tom just made it better."

Tom and Sook ultimately became nationally known for their willingness to adopt children with special needs. Both Tom's church and his employer became closely involved. Over the years Sook gained even more expertise and understanding. Often she and Tom consult with other parents who adopt special-needs children and who, like them, feel driven by the dream of creating their own "village."

Your Visioneering process has generated a short list of possibilities that stimulate and energize you. But they may not all fit neatly together into one lifetime — or perhaps not all in the same portion of your lifetime. As Nan Keohane, former president of Wellesley College and then of Duke University, has said: "I believe that if you're a woman, you can have it all. You just can't have it all at the same time." If you are not absolutely sure which vision model you would like to take for a spin first, just go ahead and pick one — any one. And start driving. Remember: You're under no obligation to stay on one course; you're merely determining whether you like the feel of this road. Taking some decisive action and getting out on the road is the only way you'll find out.

If you have a penchant for art, go to the local art gallery or museum and look around. Drop by your local college to see what art classes it may offer. Stop in at an art supply store and talk to local artists. By acting now, you make a commitment to start somewhere, even though what you test-drive may not be the make or model you'll be tooling around in six months from now.

Of course, any action is a risk. When you go through the motions of discovering what a new life might be like, you're not necessarily committing yourself to that specific life — but you're already pulling away from the one you're in now. This is why you may find yourself hesitant to get behind the wheel at this point. In your heart, you know that this would be an admission that your old life just has too many miles on it, and can't take you where you want to go.

You might still be tempted to cling to your comfortable old jalopy, even knowing that it won't get you through that string of green lights you see dangling so alluringly ahead of you. Don't worry; this is natural. You may not be ready to roll just yet. Or, like Sook, you may be so disenchanted with things as they are that you realize you have no choice but to go forward now. Either way, by pursuing Visionalysis and Visioneering, you've already put the process in gear. Sooner or later, you'll accelerate into the heady pleasures to be found in Visioncrafting.

At Your Own Risk

This kind of calculated risk-taking is comfortable for some people — they even find it exhilarating. As we discussed earlier, natural optimists have an easier time venturing into unknown territory and exploring the possibilities. Others — those of you who've had to construct your optimism by hand, step by step — may panic when the time comes to take a chance because, as the behaviorists have shown, the pain of a small loss is greater than the victory of a big gain. In fact, as Peter L.

Bernstein observed in his book about the history of risk-taking, *Against the Gods*, one's losses will always appear larger than one's gains. Don't let the fear of loss make you ignore the opportunity for gains.

But don't worry. I'm not going to try to talk you into bungee-jumping. Instead, I am going to show you how to customize risk to fit your comfort level. My advice to all gamblers is the same: Never risk more than you are willing to lose. The more you risk and win, the more you can safely bet the next time.

Taking chances does get easier with practice. To learn what your tolerance for risk is now, ask yourself these questions.

What risks have I already taken in my life?

How did I feel about taking those chances?

What level of risk keeps me awake at night?

Do I predict that my risks will turn out well?

Consulting with other people may increase your readiness to take chances. Reach out to others who share similar aspirations — if they took the risk and won, you can too. Experiment until you find a comfort level — then push yourself a little harder.

Every choice you make involves taking some chance. Once you begin to take risks, you'll discover that your world does not self-destruct if you are wrong. Instead, you learn an invaluable lesson: You can profit from wrong decisions as well as right ones. When risk-taking loses its power to intimidate, you'll become much freer to take advantage of opportunities. To expect mistakes and learn from them permits you to see yourself as human.

Experienced risk-takers are courageous, but not foolish. They always have a backup plan, a parachute they can deploy if their decision happens to be wrong and they need to bail out. They accept failure as a part of risk, and they plan for it, remaining confident because they know that success can always be just one more try away.

EXERCISE 20: READY FOR RISK?

Asking and answering the following questions in your notebook will help you take a closer look at how you evaluate risk:

1. What is my tolerance for risk: low, medium or high?
2. Do I evaluate each risk and its consequences carefully?

3. Do I see both the short-term and long-term benefits?
4. Do I use my intuition and past experience to size up risk?
5. Do I consult others about the chance I am planning to take?
6. Do I always have a backup plan if my risk doesn't pan out?
7. Is this the right time to do what I'm about to do?
8. Are there alternatives I could choose?
9. What factors (intuition, others' opinions, experience) are influencing my decision to take this risk now?
10. How would someone I admire — a mentor, predecessor, or peer — handle this risk?
11. What impact will taking this chance have on me and others over the next year?
12. What will happen to me if I don't take this chance now?

Honest answers to these questions will help you get on more comfortable terms with the risk you're contemplating. If, in proceeding through the checklist, you began to see more clearly the possible rewards of taking action, the drawbacks of taking no action, and some strategies for minimizing any uncertainties you feel, then you are well on your way to becoming a successful risk-taker.

There are no sure bets in life. The secret is to improve your odds with a calculator — the calculator being you. Find facts, search your soul, rely on past experience, consider the consequences, consult others. All of these will improve your ability to act with confidence when the time is right.

Risking a change doesn't always have to mean demanding more from yourself. Sometimes, test-driving a new dream, scary as it may seem, can actually help you trade down to a vision that is more in line with your needs and talents. Try taking something smaller for a spin: Don't try to steer a dream with way too much horsepower for you. That's exactly what happened with one of my clients, Kathleen.

KATHLEEN

Kathleen was an actress, singer, and dancer who was living in Los Angeles. She had never married; her work was her life. Over the years, Kathleen had been chosen for numerous bit parts in musicals. Yet she had always felt frustrated and resentful, because she had never landed leading roles — or even any of the many supporting parts she tried out for. Now in her late forties, Kathleen realized she was talented — and always had been. She now understood that she just wasn't outstanding enough — or lucky enough — in an extremely competitive field, to win the roles she hungered for so desperately.

After a period of feeling blue and reexamining her life, Kathleen discovered that two things were most meaningful for her: acting and being in a position of power and respect. Playing only bit parts made her feel unrecognized, unappreciated, and certainly not respected by her peers.

Fortuitously, through the connection of a friend, Kathleen was offered an opportunity to be in charge of a drama department at a private high school. After much soul-searching, she decided to accept the position — at least for the time being. It was a risk for her to leave the entertainment business, in which she had invested so much time and talent. But there was the lure of certain accomplishment and respect in a safer and less competitive role. To her own amazement, she loved her new job.

In a moment of clarity, Kathleen realized that if the opportunity to head this drama department had come earlier in her career, she would have turned it down. She wouldn't have bothered to test-drive such a modest dream, because she would have seen it as not "important" enough.

By continuing to try out for leading roles, Kathleen had been setting her sights too high. Her dissatisfaction with the lesser roles she won — even to the point of getting the blues — was a healthy reaction. Her unhappiness showed her she was on the wrong path to her vision. Finally, she allowed herself to take the risk of reaching for a more gratifying career, where her talents are appreciated and respected.

Kathleen's discontent is what motivated her. Another actress might have worked her way up through summer theaters and local productions, even considered a bit part in the "big time" the zenith of her career! But not Kathleen. She used her unhappiness to steer her in a new, more realistic direction — that turned out to be where she wanted to go all along.

TAKING YOUR OWN MEASURE

Successful Visioncrafting does not stem solely from intuition. It also involves a candid assessment of your skills, estimation of what current responsibilities you have, and conscientious design. In this section of the book, you will learn to measure your strengths and skills as they relate to your vision. We will map out a step-by-step route to your goals and set deadlines for achieving each one. Together we will chart your progress, to keep you motivated and on track. Visioncrafting is a process that helps you to clarify your intentions. When you Visioncraft you create a written action plan for your quest, a means to measure progress toward your goal. Visioncrafting also lets you assess what is working and what isn't. In other words, this is what you've been working toward all along, and you're ready. Let's try an exercise that will encourage you to start your engine.

EXERCISE 21: BE A GOAL-GETTER

The purpose of the goal-getter exercise is for you to assess where you lie along your vision's time line. I am indebted to a former client who helped design the following format to organize her aspirations. The goal-getting plan is broken down into short-term goals (STG) and long-term goals (LTG).

Divide a page of your notebook down the middle. As shown, on the left, write *STG* and *LTG*. At the top of the right-hand column, put *Progress Toward Goal*.

STG   LTG   PROGRESS TOWARD GOAL

Take some time right now to write down some of your goals that developed in your Visioneering process. You may want to use the exact words you wrote in Exercise 19, where you signed a contract that committed you to make an effort toward a certain goal. A short-term goal would be something you want to start working on immediately; a long-term goal would be a result you desire but don't yet feel ready to reach for.

As you Visioncraft, go back to this page and write down any positive steps you've taken to realize your goal. Be honest and accountable with yourself, but don't hesitate to pat yourself on the back when you make a move that's difficult or important.

To show you how this chart will work, let's say that you're an artist who needs to become more financially independent. Your short-term goal may be to give lessons in pottery-making, and your long-term goal might be to open your own school.

A first step might be to check out what sort of instruction is already available in your community. This step carries a relatively low risk — it's something you would do if you were interested in taking classes yourself. Once you've accomplished this, you can write it down on your goal-getter chart in the *Progress* column. Perhaps the next step might be to talk to some of the instructors, or even to ask if there are any current job openings. Don't be discouraged if you are rebuffed; simply write this down as another step you took toward your goal, then praise yourself.

Or say that you are a career woman who works as an insurance broker, and you want to spend more time with your children. Your short-term goal might be to do some work out of your home, so you can be there when your children arrive home from school. Your long-term goal could be establishing a home-based business related to the health insurance field.

A first step could be arranging a lunch with other local women in your field, to find out how they manage their own conflicts between work and home. This may be simply a mutual-support session, but it could provide you with some workable ideas and perhaps even valuable contacts for the business you eventually establish. It's a small step in which you have risked very little, but it's a movement toward your goal. You have taken an action related to your dream and shifted it that much closer to reality.

Return to this page in your notebook often, even if you have nothing to report. If you see no progress toward a particular goal, ask yourself why not. Don't be afraid to redefine your goals as you go along: This is an essential part of the vision process.

> *"Hell is to drift, heaven is to steer."*
> —George Bernard Shaw

In my clinical experience, most of us have an inherent fear of failure. For some it is triggered easily; for a goal-getter like Oprah Winfrey, not so easily. Our defense against possible failure is expressed in one of two ways: We choose a goal that is so easy it is certain to be achieved; or we select one that is too hard, even impossible to accomplish given our current life situation. With the first risk-aversion strategy, we are bound to succeed — but we avoid real success because we set too low a goal. At the other end of the spectrum, when a goal proves unrealistic, we then rationalize our lack of success by saying, *See? I knew I couldn't do it. I could never do that anyway — it was too difficult.*

The trick in goal setting — one that successful people use continually — is to set a goal of intermediate difficulty. You want to be challenged at just the right level — not too little, not too much — so when you do succeed, you can feel pride and say, "I did that!" You must first get to know yourself better to design realistic goals that stretch but do not break you. As Woody Allen said, "Eighty percent of success is showing up."

As Kathleen, the actress, learned, goals need to be short-term and attainable so that discouragement doesn't overtake you. Pick modest goals at first, so you enjoy a greater sense of mastery with each triumph, instead of reaching for the stars and falling short of the moon.

By the same token, if you're wishing for the moon, don't settle for the treetops. Setting goals that are too modest and too easily attainable can bring on the same sense of discouragement and disillusionment that impossible dreams generate. The dreariness of a vision that's too small for you can make success seem like failure — as it did for Lorraine.

LORRAINE

Lorraine, age forty-five, always loved medicine and chemistry. After raising two daughters, she decided to return to school to become a pharmacist. Soon after graduation, she went to work at a local Walgreen's pharmacy. Two years into her new career, she admitted to herself that she had yet to be satisfied in her chosen profession. She also felt an irrepressible restlessness. She blamed the store location, her hours, her boss. She switched pharmacies twice, but she was still dissatisfied.

One day, as Lorraine was driving to work, she heard an ad for the military: "Be all that you can be." She almost came to a dead stop in traffic and exclaimed to herself in the car, *I know what the problem is: I don't want to be a pharmacist, I want to be a physician.*

It took Lorraine a few additional undergraduate prerequisites — and several tries — to get into her state medical school. Now, at age fifty-four, she is an intern planning to specialize in radiology.

When she enrolled in pharmaceutical school, Lorraine had set her sights lower than her potential dictated; she was off the mark of her true desires. She did not take the time to dream daringly enough, or assess her visions deeply enough, and she lacked the necessary confidence to pursue medical school. Finally, Lorraine — like Kathleen — listened to her unhappiness and let it guide her to her true vocation.

> *"If you think you can, you can. If you think you can't, you're right."*
>
> —MARY KAY ASH

People often set their aspirations too low when they believe they don't have enough planning time. Your schedule is probably so tight that it barely gives you room to turn around. That doesn't mean that you should be in such a rush to find your future that you settle for the first dream that comes along.

How can you shape a vision for your new life while your old life is still around, demanding your attention and energy? The key to finding time for this crucial enterprise is derived from the same qualities that have gotten you this far: optimism and persistence. First believe that you can make room in your life for fulfillment and happiness, and then find a way to keep that commitment. Here's an exercise to get you started.

EXERCISE 22: BUY YOURSELF SOME TIME

First you'll need to go back to the chart in Exercise 21, where you spelled out exactly what you'll do to further your short-term and long-term goals. Pick a short-term goal that you haven't yet found time to pursue.

On a large piece of paper, draw a huge circle. Write, around the outside of the rim, all the activities you currently spend more than three hours a week doing — preparing meals, working, watching TV, etc. Be sure to include one category that says: *Pursuing My Dream.* Now get forty of any small item: pennies, toothpicks, poker chips, whatever you have handy.

Each item represents 2.5 percent of your waking hours, or almost three hours a week. First place them under the appropriate categories, in pie slices of various sizes. These should approximate how much time you currently spend in each activity. If you watch a movie on TV for two hours every night on work days, that's ten hours, so put three items under the category labeled *Watching TV.* Be as honest with yourself as possible. This pie chart represents your current schedule — a graphic representation of how you allot time each week.

Now move some of your game pieces into the segment below *Pursuing My Dream.* Be realistic about choosing them from categories where you can get away with devoting fewer hours. Can you make time for one item (almost three hours) by getting help with the laundry on Saturdays?

Once you have found a way to unlock even a few hours, you can extend this chart to the following week. For example, say your vision is to go to law school. Begin by filling in how much time next week you will spend gathering information. Write a contract to yourself that says "Beginning next Saturday, instead of going to the mall, I will go to the library and research local law schools."

Start with small tasks. Don't get too ambitious or make promises you can't keep. Schedule for only a week or two, so you can readjust according to your actual progress and maximize the next step's chances for success. Be flexible. Break your goal down into small, achievable steps that are challenging and fun. Remember Goldilocks's porridge: not too hot, not too cold, just right. And, most important, reward yourself with a special treat for each step taken.

ACHIEVE TASK MASTERY

One trick successful entrepreneurs use to free up time for themselves is to list all the tasks that don't require their expertise — i.e., projects anyone can do. Then they hire and train someone to do them.

Another strategy they use to stay on the track of their destiny is to make a list of what they like to do best and also what they would just as soon give up because it is not as fulfilling. You can unlock time by making a list of tasks you like least and that you would like to be relieved of so you can pursue your own goals. Then make a list of what each family member is capable of. A child need not be very old to set the table, for instance, or put clean laundry away in drawers.

Mary Kay Ash, the successful founder of Mary Kay Cosmetics, developed a plan for her employees to help them achieve their goals. She feels it's critical that they wake up each morning with their daily goals nearby. Mary Kay gives her salespeople sheets of paper entitled "The Six Most Important Things To Do Tomorrow." She tells her employees to leave this list on their night table and recommends putting what they most dread doing at the top of the list. The task is to cross off each goal as it is done. Any task not finished at the end of the day is carried over to the top of the next day's list.

An interesting facet of the Mary Kay Cosmetics method is its emphasis on tackling the least desirable tasks first. It's human nature to put off what we dread. But if we can manage to meet those problems head on, we acquire a momentum that is almost unstoppable. Ask yourself whether part of the reason you're having trouble isolating enough time for your Visioncrafting research is that old red light we've talked about before: fear.

Are you going to feel some nervousness as you explore various methods for realizing your vision? You bet. Fear is a normal emotion you will experience when you step out of a familiar environment or interrupt your schedule. You will feel apprehensive — perhaps outright frightened — while doing something new, or even merely educating yourself about the possibility of doing something different.

In this instance, the trick is to *steer in the direction of the skid:* Recognize the fear, acknowledge it, accept it as part of the process. Ironically, what we fear most is often that which we find most thrilling and gratifying. Remember as a child when you were dared to do something, or felt peer pressure to do what your friend or group were doing? Remember how even though you were scared, you did it anyway — perhaps foolishly — because other incentives overrode your fear? You already possess this skill, the just-do-it skill. You only need to bring it out of hiding.

As you're traveling down what looks like a fairly smooth route to your goal and anxiety begins to rain down on you like an afternoon shower, resist the urge to pull over until the storm passes. Go full speed ahead with those emotions; they can be a source of strength. Relabel your anxieties as "stimulating," "energizing," and "elating." Suddenly you're as poised and determined as Anna in *The King and I,* when she whistles a happy tune — "and every single time, the happiness in the tune convinces me that I'm — not afraid!"

Another method for handling your fears requires that you begin with the least daunting ones and work your way upward. Here's an exercise that helps you master fears by starting with those at the bottom.

EXERCISE 23: THE LADDER OF FEARS
Rank your list of fears from the bottom (lower anxiety producers) to the top (the scary stuff). This technique handles fears through the therapeutic process of desensitization.

Go to a quiet place. Close your eyes and introduce into your imagination something — anything — that brings an absolute sense of relaxation, something that you are totally comfortable with. This might be an image of rocking in a hammock on a summer afternoon, or lying on a secluded beach, or reposing in a hot tub. Whatever makes you exhale with a long "ahhhhh . . ." will do.

Next, let your mind focus on the least fear-arousing item on your list. Breathe deeply, then exhale slowly, keeping your eyes closed. Bring your mind back to that most relaxed of places and restore the tranquility. Alternate back and forth from the fearful image to the secure, soothing one, until you stay relaxed in thoughts about your former fear. When you have managed to relieve the least intimidating item, move up the ladder using the same sequence. If you are struggling while doing this alone, recruit a trusted friend who can help you develop this useful skill.

This method can be called upon if you are in the midst of pursuing your goal and some seemingly menacing step awaits you — like breaking the news to your partner or family that you want to go to college or open a catalog sales business.

With a reduced sense of dread derived from the relaxation exercise, you can now see yourself not as a victim of the fear, but rather as a survivor — someone with a different future and additional options. You are now ready to get on stage.

The next step is to mentally role-play through the fear. In this one-act play, try to anticipate what might happen if your fear is realized. To use the example of a woman telling her family that she wants to go back to college, perhaps she might anticipate her children would laugh at her ambition and tell her that it's out of the question.

Then develop a plan and visualize putting it into play — literally deciding what actions you will take and the words you will use with others — while remaining relaxed. The mother who wants to go to school could counter her children's jeers and objections by demonstrating to them how much she's already learned about the subject she wants to study. In her one-act play, she can see herself impressing them with the depth of her research and preparation.

TEST THOSE ASSUMPTIONS

Fear isn't the only obstacle that can prevent you from test-driving your vision. Faulty assumptions can just as easily block your progress during this survey stage. For instance, you may convince yourself that your local community college doesn't accept people your age or permit taking classes unless you are enrolled in a degree program; or you might assume that your spouse would oppose your plans. That's what testing is about — finding the *real* limits. What may appear to be a massive, impenetrable roadblock may be just one of those orange plastic cones that are easily removed or driven around. One thing's for sure: You'll never get anywhere if you don't find out.

You can be especially vulnerable to false assumptions when you're deciding between those two major thoroughfares, achieving and nurturing. If you're considering a path that you feel goes against what those around you expect, you may be stymied by the assumption that they'll disapprove. Many nurturers who want to become achievers, for instance, are sensitive to this sort of imagined resistance. But I remember one woman, Marilyn, who made the same false assumptions about her husband's reaction to her shift from one nurturing role to another, when she wanted to return to a caretaking role after her children were grown.

M A R I L Y N

Marilyn, remarried at forty-seven, watched anxiously as her son Stephen, age twenty-four, struggled to find himself. He had been in and out of several jobs since graduating from college three years before. "I wish I could help him get some direction, but every time I want to give him money or advice, Ron, my husband, tells me to back off. What I would really like is to have Stephen come live with us so I could give him some tender, loving care and guidance. But Ron would never allow it. Maybe it's unfair for me to even ask him."

I encouraged Marilyn to talk to Ron. Maybe if he saw the merit in her wanting to help Stephen, he wouldn't object. If she developed a plan and presented it calmly and realistically, I suggested, perhaps her belief that Ron wouldn't cooperate would turn out to be unfounded.

Surprisingly to Marilyn, Ron was more than willing to consider her wishes, as long as they were clear about where her son would live in the house, what the ground rules would be, and how long Stephen would stay.

Marilyn assumed that Ron was an obstacle to her plan. And she felt uncomfortable asking for his cooperation. To her delight, she discovered he was not a red light at all, because she followed the plan I had outlined for her. She defined her idea thoroughly, broke it down into doable steps, then presented her vision in a reasonable way, with room for compromise and restructuring. If she hadn't been willing to set aside her false assumptions about Ron's reluctance, she never would have developed such an effective plan for helping her son.

Whether Marilyn's relationship with Ron sounds like yours, or your partner is more openly generous and supportive, you may still experience the guilt Marilyn felt when she asked for one of her needs to be met. Guilt is a "mind trap," a straitjacket that ties you up and makes it difficult for you to think calmly and logically about your goals.

As a woman, ever since the birth of humanity, you have been expected to be a caretaker. Only in the past few decades has our society made more choices available to you than just providing for others. Even today, old cultural obligations linger and may stir up a conflict in you between caretaking others versus meeting your own needs. This struggle reveals itself as anxiety or fear and explains why, when you are cruising along on your quest, you feel compelled to stop at green lights or you encounter only red ones.

When you try to escape from this conditioning, and embark on a route that is new for you, you are often hampered by your own mind traps of guilt and also by society's judgments. Your mind's goal, which it valiantly tries to achieve, is the survival of these preprogrammed and learned ideas and opinions. Your job is to unlock these mind traps and set yourself free.

It Never Hurts to Ask

One way to help yourself escape from your own traps is to embark on what is called *informational interviewing.* I suggest you make an appointment with someone who can help you progress toward your goal. You are not trying to get a job or be accepted by a school; you are simply seeking to collect information that they have and you don't. First consider people you admire. Then identify others already engaged in some form of what you think you'd like to do. Now, go ahead: Call them up. Ask whether you can just sit down and chat with them about what they do — and what you are considering.

Informational interviews are not as intimidating as they sound. The roles are reversed; you are the interviewer and you ask the questions. You can relax and enjoy yourself, because there's no need to impress. Hopefully, this person will help you brainstorm. He or she is not assessing your skills or judging you. When you meet, open the conversation by asking your interviewee first about his or her work — whether it is enjoyable and challenging. This will provide some perspective from which to interpret the interview. Next, let the person in on your goals and skills. Ask, "What would you do in my position? Where would you go for information? Whom would you talk to? What would you read?"

People are usually flattered and sympathetic when approached for an informational interview. And remember, if you are turned down by someone who doesn't have time or can't be bothered, don't let it faze you. Consider the request as just another step you've taken in your research. Congratulate yourself, and go on to the next person.

What if, when testing out your vision, just barely learning the first steps to the new dance — you stumble? There's always the chance that an informational interview will be discouraging or disappointing. If you fear trying something new, you will view this falter as a disaster, when in fact it is a tiny setback. How many times have you overestimated the negative outcome of something? Blown it way out of proportion? Looking back, you've probably said to yourself, "At the moment, it seemed like the end of the world, but now I realize it wasn't so bad."

E R I N

Occasionally, what seems like a setback can turn out to be a green light in disguise. Erin had worked for a computer skills training company for three years as a technical editor when she was laid off in what her company called a "right-sizing." Her shock and dismay, on the day when two executives called her into an office and told her she was unemployed, were overwhelming.

Picking up the pieces, Erin accepted her former employers' offer of career counseling. After a couple of months, with the encouragement of her two best friends, who were both entrepreneurs, Erin decided to start her own business. Her risk-taking paid off: Four years later, she now has a flourishing writing career and a business that employs two others. She did what any choreographer would instruct you to do when you stumble: Make it part of the dance.

When you experience a setback, you must find the next green light and keep driving. Never, ever quit or sacrifice your goal when you're feeling afraid, disheartened, or dejected. When you have slept on it, have regained some perspective, and are well past the particular mud puddle that blurred your vision for a bit, then you can consider retailoring your goal.

> *"I am not discouraged, because every wrong attempt discarded is another step found."*
> —THOMAS EDISON

Pulling into a rest stop to examine a map for road hazards ahead may not sound very appealing at this point in the journey. It's unpleasant to dwell on what could go wrong, but it is necessary to keep you headed in the right direction. Here's an exercise to help you locate perils along your way — to make the driving less stressful.

EXERCISE 24: ROUGH PAVEMENT AHEAD

Make two columns on a page in your notebook. At the top of the left column, write *What If;* at the top of the right column, *My Solution.* Now imagine everything that could possibly go wrong. Write as fast as you can for as long as you can. Include anything from the absolute worst to whatever is bearable, but not desirable. A solution for avoiding these road hazards may pop into your head immediately: If so, put it in the right column.

Now go back over your list. More slowly and deliberately, consider what you would do in the case of each and every flat tire or pothole or breakdown.

For example, when Erin was thinking about starting her business, she wondered what would happen if she found she didn't like the financial strains, the long hours, and the buck-stops-here responsibility of being an entrepreneur. She discovered tremendous relief in articulating the obvious solution: If she didn't like her life as an entrepreneur, she would go out and find a job. As obvious as this sounds, having a backup plan empowered her to pursue her goal with enormous optimism. She gave herself permission to dislike her choice.

"You've got to go out on a limb sometimes because that's where all the fruit is."
—WILL ROGERS

chapter 9

Tuning Up
Your
Plan

This test-driving phase — the Visioncrafting that is so necessary before you hit the road for real — will be an anxious time for you. Maybe you're sitting awake at night, your heart pumping out desperate alarms at the radical changes you've been thinking about. *What if this doesn't work?* you ask yourself, over and over. *What if I can't do this after all? There's so much that can go wrong.*

This is the time to remind yourself that optimism and persistence will see you through — along with a third quality that you should never leave home without: flexibility. The most likely opportunity for your plan to fail has nothing to do with any shortcomings you perceive in yourself. If your vision drives you in the wrong direction, it will likely be because you're clinging to it too rigidly — because you are unwilling to modify, amend, even overhaul it to allow for adverse driving conditions.

As you pursue your vision, you should remain ready to revise your original mission statement. What you may discover is that you are as hesitant to change as those around you. You may have done an admirable job of bringing a long-held dream into focus, even testing it out by experimenting and information gathering. You are infinitely proud — and you should be — of the meticulous blueprint you have created. You now have a road-ready plan — or so you think.

Remember that movie you made back in Chapter Seven, in which you were the producer, the director, and the star? You prepared the entire script, stage sets, and props. You even rehearsed it over and over. Did you think the performance would be exactly like the rehearsal? Or that one take would be the same as the next, or the next? No, your pursuit has its own set of influences that can alter its course—entirely beyond your control. If you are inflexible and unwilling to learn from wrong turns, you may end up heading directly into traffic on a one-way street.

Whenever you buy a new car, the manufacturer tells you to bring it back after the first few thousand miles, to make sure it's tuned properly. By the time you've bought your third or fourth car, you're able to take in stride any small, irritating defects that emerge right away; you've learned that imperfections are to be expected, that adjustments and troubleshooting are part of the process.

Why should you expect your own dream vehicle to be more flawless than the cars that are turned out on an assembly line in Detroit? The design may be ingenious, even inspired; but only a thorough road test will reveal the thousand-and-one eventualities you couldn't possibly have foreseen.

The more prepared you are for your Visionmobile to stall, the better you'll be able to resist those powerful urges to turn around and drive back to familiar surroundings—to the status quo. When you find yourself daydreaming wistfully about that old clunker you traded in for this shiny new Visionmobile—how safe it was, how predictable—it will help you reassure yourself that all your second adulthood needs is a little tune-up.

When the desire to beat a retreat to the past overwhelms you, you're making the classic mistake of seeing yourself as a helpless passenger, not as the owner-operator of your vision. As discouraged as you might feel, tell yourself that these urges to quit will come and go. Wait these doubts out until you can be objective about their core message. Meanwhile, while your dream is in the shop, take a break from your journey by doing something familiar and fun.

Remember, no one succeeds at everything. Not every one of Meryl Streep's movies is a box-office smash. Setbacks are not a sign of failure; they are an inseparable part of the process of change. Best of all, they have a silver lining: the opportunity to learn. You may even make several more unsuccessful attempts before leaping over a particular hurdle. Successful plans are edited, fine-tuned versions of unsuccessful ones. There's only one way to find out what works, and that's to try it.

"If you want to increase your success rate, double your failures."

—Tom Watson, IBM

Successful people take optimism to its absolute limit by seeing failure as enabling. Defeat affords them the opportunity to revise and perfect the plan. They're not afraid to analyze what went wrong and devise strategies to overcome that loss the next time. They ask themselves certain questions when something doesn't go as planned, or if they don't achieve their goal. Try asking yourself these questions when you have a setback:

What preceded my failure? How can I avoid it in the future? Could I have been more prepared for or responded better to this circumstance?

Am I expecting too much? Are the steps I plan too ambitious, and do they need to be smaller to better balance challenge with success?

Am I trying to do too much too quickly? Do I need to modify my timetable?

What barriers can I remove before taking this step again?

What can this experience teach me?

What celebration shall I plan when I succeed?

You've seen that sign on the side mirrors of cars: "Objects are closer than they appear." Looking at the past is exactly like that: Once you've solved a problem and put it behind you, it simply doesn't loom as large in your vision. The same type of optical illusion occurs — but in reverse — with the problems that still lie ahead of you: Setbacks will always appear larger than they are, until you've managed to get past them.

When things go wrong in a pursuit we care deeply about, often we overinterpret and magnify the outcome out of its true proportion. Shove aside your negative self-chatter; remind yourself of your progress so far. Then congratulate yourself on the distance you have traveled already. This will make a minor setback appear as it really is — something you can shrug off and toss away. Now you can see: It is not the lapse that is important, but how you perceive and correct it.

Of course, not every setback is minor. There is a possibility that you might come up against a mountain you can't get past. Regardless of how hard we try, some challenges are insurmountable. Wisdom lies in recognizing these obstacles, accepting them, and — most importantly — resetting your sights toward a new, attainable target. Repeated failures, without a break to make adjustments, will only erode your self-esteem and make you feel like quitting. So, with your optimism still fully in forward gear, say to yourself, *Okay. This might be beyond my reach — but now I'll reach for something closer.*

THE SCHOOL OF HARD KNOCKS

A story in the *Wall Street Journal* by Stephanie N. Mehta featured two Chicago women, both forty-one, who were stalled in their quest to secure $2 million in financing to launch a day spa for stressed-out executive women. After working on proposals and stock offerings for two years, the women were still half a million dollars short of their goal, thanks to a thriving stock market that made potential investors reluctant to divert their funds toward a small business start-up. Rather than embark on a venture that was undercapitalized, or alter their vision beyond recognition, the women said they were ready to abandon the project if they didn't raise the money by a certain deadline.

Still, the women were optimistic enough to see their failed quest as a learning experience. "I can't imagine learning as much in graduate school as I have in the last two years," one of them told the *Journal*.

> "He who has never failed somewhere . . .
> cannot be great. Failure is the true test of
> greatness."
> —HERMAN MELVILLE, *MOBY DICK*

The road you are traveling to your chosen destination has plenty of potholes; your emotional shock-absorbers depend on your ability to see the bumps coming and get over them gently. Optimists see untoward events as temporary, avoidable, unlikely to repeat themselves. They think in terms of external causes. Pessimists, on the other hand, generalize the jarring to describe their whole life; they blame themselves for bad road conditions, and they see those conditions as beyond repair.

Let's say that you have opened your own business and handled a few jobs. Then, on one bid, you underestimate the cost of the work and you lose money. An optimist says, *Well, I'll never do that again. Let me see if I can figure out why this happened so I can avoid it in the future.* A pessimist says, *Oh, I'll never learn to estimate properly; I don't know why I ever attempted this. I've never been good with numbers, no wonder I lost money. I'll only lose more money next time.*

Interestingly, the same thinking applies to good fortune. When a new business is doing well, optimists see the success as permanent. They attribute the good fortune to the totality of their life circumstances — and they take credit for their accomplishments. An optimist will say, *I paid my dues and now it's paying off. My whole life is going well for me now. I saw the opportunity and I grasped it.*

But a pessimist is skeptical of such a happy ending, seeing any success as only temporary. Any small victory is attributed to luck, other people's efforts, or a few coincidences rather than to skill or persistence. A pessimist might respond to the winning of a profitable contract by saying, *Well, that was lucky — but we'll never get another company's contract. Things may be fine here at this business, but my family life is compromised. We would never have gotten that contract if I hadn't stayed up all night preparing the proposal.*

Don't be afraid to enjoy the pleasurable, trouble-free parts of your journey as what they are: evidence of a Visionmobile that's well-tuned and running on all its cylinders. If you're forced to pull off the road later — as everyone must, from time to time — your diagnostic tuning session will go more smoothly, because you'll be equipped with an intimate working knowledge of how wonderful it feels when your timing is right on the money.

*D*on't Be a
*R*oad
*W*orrier

A s you merge into the traffic-clogged road to success, you will
find plenty to worry about: *Will I know which way to turn at
the next major intersection? Will I have the courage to keep
going when I see a green light? Will my brakes fail if I need to slow down
suddenly, to figure out which direction to take? Will I be able to see all the
road hazards and avoid them? Will I accelerate too fast, leaving something — or someone — behind?*

Worry can be a thief of your time, stealing away hours and never
making restitution. However, when practiced in moderation, worrying can actually be productive. It compels us to act on what worries
us. Deadlines are a perfect example: We fuss and fume and procrasti-
nate until it's almost too late to make the deadline, then throw all that
pent-up energy into a fireworks display of action that explosively
completes the task.

Worry and anxiety are also helpful if, like a warning light on your
dashboard, they signal to you that something is wrong — that perhaps
you should slow down and proceed with caution.

Anxiety and worry played an important survival role for our ancestors. Just as physical pain can be a useful signal that something is not
right in your body, worry can be your early warning system when your
emotions are out of kilter. Unfortunately, worry — like those mysterious aches and pains everyone feels from time to time — can kick in
when you don't need or want it. And then you can't seem to stop it.

When worry accumulates too much in the mind, the overload shorts out your circuits and shuts you down into learned helplessness — the giving-up response we discussed at the beginning of this book. When that happens, the feedback loop completes itself between mind and body, and you experience physical symptoms like headaches, an irritable bowel, backaches, loss of interest in sex, high blood pressure, or depression. And, it goes without saying, none of this is what you need right now, right in the middle of your Visioncrafting!

If you find yourself lying awake nights obsessing about your new venture, or expending inordinate energy in vicious circles of ruminating that keep leading to the same conclusion, ask yourself, *What evidence do I have that what I am worrying about will come true?* You'll need all the facts, so search out what the possible consequences will be if your worry *is* well-founded; you may discover you have exaggerated the outcome. Apply the adage about knowing the difference between things you can change and those you cannot. Don't waste time fretting about something that is beyond your control or responsibility.

A common worry for anyone contemplating change is money: *Where will I find the finances to implement my idea?* A good way to analyze this problem is to jot down all the activities in your life that require money: housing, food, clothing, college tuition, child care, hobbies, sports, vacations, entertainment. Now write out a time line of one- and five-year increments. This shows you how your current expenses will ebb and flow with whatever obligations you might have. It can help you to pick the best window of opportunity to pursue your dream.

If you have a tendency to worry excessively, here's a technique to help you gain better control over it. I devised it for my clients to take the sting out of all those worries that swarm and buzz in their brains.

EXERCISE 25: THE WORRY WORKOUT
Allot fifteen to twenty minutes each day for exercising your worries. Start the session by deliberately conjuring up any fears you have about pursuing your new vision. Don't judge whether the proposed problem is immediate or in the future. Practice fretting as hard as you can. Then give yourself a *worry waiver,* a time-out from worrying. At first your worry waiver may only last ten minutes. But this is a good start. You might then expand this session in increments of ten minutes until you have reached a time block you feel comfortable with. Repeat this

session daily. You will find that your worries, like sticks of gum, will lose their flavor from overchewing.

When you sit down for your daily worry workout, have your notebook and pencil ready to write down any solutions you may come up with. In describing your worry, ask yourself the following questions:

What is the likelihood that what I am worried about will actually happen?

What are the worst things that could occur if my fear comes true?

What are the pluses if my concern happens?

How would I deal with the worst-case scenario?

How can I plan to prevent or eliminate the worry?

One of my clients, Jennifer, aged forty-one, ruminated constantly that she would never get pregnant. Because her husband had undergone a vasectomy, she fretted that it couldn't be reversed. She worried that if she did manage to get pregnant, the baby would be retarded. Instead of allowing her to enjoy her honeymoon and early months of marriage, these thoughts dominated Jennifer's existence.

I counseled her to try the strategy of postponing her worries until a designated time each day. During her worry workout, she trained herself to list all the best- and worst-case consequences that could stem from her concerns. Then, for each worry, she developed a specific alternative explanation. For example, when she worried about the vasectomy reversal, she now had a countering response: "With all the latest microsurgery techniques, there is a very good chance that a reversal will succeed." She also negated that apprehension by researching other workable solutions, such as artificial insemination and adoption. In other words, she formulated a backup plan that gave her worries an excuse to relax.

In my experience with thousands of clients, many people who overworry and then review their worries years later, are amused at how few of their fears ever materialized — or if they did, how inconsequential they really were!

> "*I am an old man and have known a great many troubles, but most of them never happened.*"
>
> —MARK TWAIN

If you are actively worrying about a decision you need to make, sometimes the only way to end your obsessing is to go ahead and decide. Once you make that crucial turn at the intersection, it's easier to keep driving toward your goal. And who says you can't turn around and come back, if you discover later that you've gone the wrong way?

SIT UP AND RELAX

Here are some other tips for derailing the worry cycle, adapted from an article entitled "Beat Stress All Day" by Perry Garfinkle, in the January/February 1997 issue of *Men's Health:*

1. When worries keep you tossing and turning, try to dream your way out of them. A study of the dreams of 656 athletes revealed that their waking performance was directly related to their dream performance. In other words, it's literally true that if you can dream it, you can do it.

2. One strategy to avoid helplessness in adverse circumstances is to take control to whatever extent you can. "If the train stops between stations," advises Garfinkle, "and no one announces why, find a conductor and ask what's up and how long the train will be delayed." Even if you don't get any answers, taking whatever action you can will bring you some relief.

3. In a high-pressure situation, remind yourself of other times when you've dealt with just as much pressure and succeeded.

4. Listen to music, and let its charms soothe the savage breast of your worries. It doesn't matter what kind of music, as long as it lightens your mood.

5. Be sure to eat your fruits and vegetables. It's true! Certain foods that are low in protein and high in flavonoids — onions, apples, broccoli, tea, and grapes — help to lower your adrenaline level and counteract that stressful feeling.

6. Don't set up your risk-taking as a win-or-lose situation. Establish in your mind how much risk is comfortable, so you don't have to think in terms of loss.

7. After you've tackled some concerns, give yourself some cool-down time. Spend leisure hours with your children — they're actually good for your health!— or in communing with nature, which slows your respiration and cardiac rates.

8. Breathe deeply. Relax and then tense and then loosen your muscles. If a worry swims into your mind, press the button on an imaginary remote control, and change the channel of your thoughts until you find a more relaxing program.

Finally, you can mount one of the most persuasive arguments against your own worries when you tell yourself: *Let me do it my way.* Remember that Frank Sinatra song, "My Way"? — "Regrets; I've had a few, but then again, too few to mention." When *Fortune* magazine interviewed seven women whom they deemed the best in their fields, they found a surprise: None of these women had deliberately planned their careers. In fact, they defied conventional women's norms and broke every imaginable rule advised by career counselors and human resource experts.

These are women who don't even try to blend into corporate culture, nor do they complain when it works against them. They don't act or think like men, nor do they play the corporate game. They don't wear suits or play golf. In other words, their style is their own and it works magnificently. They do it their way. Contrary to the single, childless stereotype of a successful female executive some years back, all seven of these women have children. They make no attempt to hide their femininity. In fact, they flaunt it — to tremendous advantage. These are four-wheel-drive women — undaunted by going off-road. These seven executives celebrate the diversity of their life experiences. They explain that their many roles serve to make them multifaceted. They contend that you might not know the "right" road until you are on it. As one of them puts it, her job is but one phase of her life's journey — and she may venture next in any direction on the compass.

All have suffered adversity, including discrimination, suspicions that they had slept their way to success, refusals by some men to work with them, and clients who dismissed their ideas solely because they were women. One woman recommends that you don't allow these inevitable occurrences to discourage you by taking them personally. I agree with her: If you take others' judgments or put-downs to heart, your confidence will diminish, your ego will become defensive, and you'll lose focus on your primary goal.

That's not to say that these women do not draw the line when it needs to be drawn. One of them tells of a high-powered meeting where she was the only woman present. The new owner of her company's U.S. division asked her to get him some coffee. Her reply was: "Yeah, I'll get you coffee if you'll Xerox these papers for me." He laughed, and so did she, at this spontaneous sign of the times. All seven women say they find a sense of humor invaluable.

> *"No matter what happens, keep on beginning and failing. Each time you fail, start all over again, and you will grow stronger until you find that you have accomplished a purpose — not the one you began with, perhaps, but one you will be glad to remember."*
>
> —ANNE SULLIVAN,
> TEACHER OF HELEN KELLER

FIND YOUR FLOW

If you are like many women, your life becomes more predictable in proportion to your ability to plan ahead and maintain a schedule. I can hear the collective laughter of mothers everywhere when I say that — particularly women who are currently raising young children or infants.

Mothers have a distinct advantage when it comes to chasing dreams: Your experience with the ever-shifting waves of chaos that only children can generate is terrific preparation. You already know how to go with the flow when nothing seems to turn out as you planned it. And you know that the confusion would be even worse if you hadn't laid out an excellent plan in the first place.

Flow is the term used by University of Chicago psychologist Dr. Mihaly Csikszentmihalyi (pronounced chick-SENT-mehi) to describe the mental zone where you lose awareness of what you are doing. Have you ever been doing something, looked at your watch, and wondered whether it was broken because time had passed so quickly? This is flow. In the business of living to the fullest, you lose your perspective on time and yourself. Flow enhances well-being and your sense of mastery. To experience flow, and go with it, you must find challenge and meaning, and latch onto pursuits that make the most of your abilities. Csikszentmihalyi identified four integral aspects to going with the flow:

1. Set goals.
2. Immerse yourself in the activity.
3. Pay attention to what is happening.
4. Enjoy the immediate experience.

Do you see the resemblance to what we've been discussing in regard to Visioncrafting? When you are truly in sync with your quest, and going with the flow, small worries will fall away from you and your direction will reveal itself almost magically. You are in flow when you operate from intention, doing the things that are meaningful to you and that reinforce your sense of mastery. So *go with your personal flow.*

This isn't always easy, especially when something happens to interrupt the flow, and you have to stop and think about it — just as when you're riding a horse, you may sometimes feel as if it were a separate animal with notions of its own about where it wants to gallop. The critical element to keep in mind is that there is more than one right direction to go in to reach your goal. Continual trial and error and course corrections will be necessary.

Stay open to where this horse — your personal flow — takes you, even if you feel you are not always in control of the reins. It's okay to roam. One woman, the co-inventor of what is now an internationally marketed product, said, "At times, we just let the business go where it wanted; it seemed to have a life of its own."

Visioncrafting is the vital connection between fantasizing and realizing your dreams. You can fantasize about taking a Mediterranean cruise, standing on a balcony, ordering room service, getting a massage, and sitting outside at an Italian cafe watching the boats pull into the harbor. But putting these plans into play is another story. *You suddenly have to face decisions you never considered: What cruise line should I choose? Which particular ship? How long a vacation do I want? What deck do I want to be on? How much can I realistically spend? Where exactly do I want to go?*

You might even find yourself changing your mind. What might have sounded good in the beginning now seems less appealing. Why? Probably because as you accumulated more information, your preferences came into focus.

Realizing your long-term life's mission is no different. First you need a vision, then you need a plan, and finally you need revisions . . . and more revisions . . . of that plan, until you have a clear focus.

That focus is the sign that you've completed your Visioncrafting successfully. You test-drove your ideas until you saw clearly where you wanted to go and how you might get there. Now you're ready, at last, to set off on your journey — knowing in your heart that whatever challenges you find along the way, you have the tools and the talent to master them.

Summary: Visioncrafting

1. Test-drive any and all possible dreams, even if you're uncertain whether they're what you will commit to for the long term.
2. If you fear taking the risk of testing your vision, opt for small steps that make the venture more comfortable for you. Don't gamble more than you can afford to lose.
3. Design realistic goals that stretch but do not break you.
4. Find time to chase your dream by carving up your goals into digestible, bite-sized pieces — and by deciding what part of your current obligations you can ask for help with.
5. When fear and anxiety threaten to deter you from your route, just steer in the direction of the skid, confident that you can straighten out your course fairly soon.
6. Don't let false assumptions place imaginary obstacles in your path. Find out whether they're based on reality, or merely mind traps.
7. Use informational interviews to see your dream through more experienced eyes.
8. Keep an eye out for possible road hazards ahead, and have an emergency backup plan prepared in advance.
9. Learn to take start-up failures in stride, and use them as opportunities to fine-tune your vision.
10. Give yourself permission to worry — even setting aside a time each day to do so — and then dismiss any worries that prove to be unfounded. Use backup plans to neutralize the worries.
11. Go with your own personal flow. Give yourself up to the momentum of the ride, remaining in control of the wheel but confidently — and optimistically — expecting the unexpected.

part

VISIONAVIGATING

*B*ring 'Em
*A*long for the
*R*ide

JULIA

When her grown children carried that cake into the family room, it sparkled with tiny blazes. Fifty candles crowded its crown, one for each of her years.

Everyone laughed, then nibbled away at the various desserts John had personally selected from the caterers for his wife Julia's fiftieth birthday. Julia was delighted. Two of her sisters and her three children had flown in from all over the country. Her youngest child had even brought her baby — the first grandchild. Everyone seemed relaxed and joyful.

Yet the next morning, they awoke to the sound of Julia running the vacuum cleaner. It seemed that no matter how much the caterers had promised, they couldn't manage to clean the house the way she liked. "I should start a cleaning service," she mumbled between dustings. No one paid any attention; it was just Mom mumbling.

But at dinner, she mentioned it again.

"Don't be silly," her husband John said. "You've been cleaning our house for over twenty years. You want to do that in your fifties too? That's like a mail carrier going for a walk on a day off!"

"You should be traveling," the first son said, "now that Dad's semiretired."

"You should sell the house and get a smaller place in the city," the first daughter advised.

"You should visit me more often and baby-sit," the youngest daughter pleaded.

Julia just nodded.

Weeks went by. She went to the movies. She planned a vacation for the spring. Once she even scanned the yellow pages under "house-cleaning" just to see how many companies were listed. She mentioned her idea again to her husband. His reply: "You don't have the time."

Her mother said, "Ugh — cleaning."

Her oldest sister said, "A business? At your age?"

Her other sister said, "What do you know about professional cleaning?"

Do any of these disparaging remarks sound familiar? Maybe when you've expressed your ideas, they have elicited the same kinds of dis-heartening responses from the people you look to for support. Unfortunately, many women are too easily discouraged by the nega-tive feedback from their families.

Let's face it; most families don't like change. They're invested in keeping the status quo; they feel fearful and threatened. Julia's family was no exception — but she succeeded in overcoming their doubts. How? She fulfilled four crucial requirements:

1. Her idea was realistic. She gathered information to support it. She created a plan consisting of small, attainable steps, complete with time lines.
2. She adopted an optimistic style of thinking, to surmount the doubts expressed by her family and herself.
3. She persisted.
4. She believed in herself and her idea. She envisioned herself succeeding.

What made Julia so successful was that her idea tapped into her already existing abilities, and filled a need in her community. And she was resourceful in taking modest steps to test-drive her dream.

LEARNING BY WATCHING

Julia's information gathering began when she called several of the cleaning companies in the yellow pages and made arrangements for them to clean a portion of her own house. She watched them work — and she also watched the clock. She wrote down what cleaning sup-plies they used, how they cleaned — and what tasks they neglected or declined to do.

This last, she found, amounted to quite a long list — no bed making, no doing of laundry, no polishing wood floors, no cleaning draperies, no dumping wastebaskets, no dish washing, no taking every knickknack down off the shelves to dust. In short, they did *none* of the things most customers want done — and hate doing themselves.

Julia's intuition had been correct: Plenty of ways existed to surpass the competition. Armed with this information, she was conscious of a glow of anticipation. Her dream had begun to grow wings — now she couldn't get it off her mind.

However, Julia continued to garner nothing but discouragement from her family:

"Forget it," her husband said. "We've got tickets to London."

"Forget it," her sisters said. "Who wants to do what they hate doing at home? Besides, there isn't any money in it."

Julia thought to herself, *Well, corporations have money. Country clubs have money. People who throw big parties and need competent cleanup crews have money.*

The more they blocked her ambitions, the more confused she became. It was at this point that Julia came to see me.

I was impressed by how far Julia had come on her own. Her Visionalysis was a recognition of her fiftieth birthday as the starting point for her second adulthood. She Visioneered by identifying a business that tapped her experience, interests, and capabilities. And she had even begun Visioncrafting — by cleverly checking out the competition in her own home. I challenged her to take the next step: to come up with a painless way to test the market potential for her services.

She decided to place an ad in the paper: "CLEANING—JUST THE WAY YOU LIKE IT."

Within six weeks, Julia had a business.

"Oh, can I help?" beseeched one of her sisters, who was surprised to witness such an enviable transformation. But it was too late: Julia had already hired another person to work alongside her.

That was three years ago. Today Julia owns and operates a profitable and respected house and office cleaning service in her town. And she didn't sacrifice her all-important family life to pursue her independence. Instead, she brought her family along on her journey — and gained their esteem and admiration in the process.

PLAYING TO HER STRENGTHS

How did she do it? What was her secret? Although her transition from nurturing to achieving occurred rapidly, it wasn't without effort and calculation on Julia's part. She had to learn and practice some new habits to achieve success.

First she took inventory of her existing skills. She didn't dream about opening a store that sold tambourines, nor did she aspire to become a rocket scientist. She didn't have the knowledge base for this, nor did she have the time needed to acquire it. Julia went about learning the cleaning business without having to go back to school — she merely hired the companies and paid close attention. After seeing them work, she confirmed her hunch that she could do the same thing, only better — and with her existing abilities.

She also learned that the need to have "extra" household cleaning jobs done was not unusual; other women — and companies — wanted relief from the same chores. Having this information built Julia's feelings of mastery — many of her intuitions about operating cleaning services were turning out to be right.

Julia also practiced optimism, maintaining belief in herself, since those close to her were not supportive. Julia didn't *think* she could do it, she *knew* she could do it. Yes, she had never run a business. Yes, she had never hired people. Yes, she had never priced out jobs. But deep down, she knew this was a *possible* dream.

Another reason Julia succeeded was because she cultivated the habit of persistence. Remember the little red hen we admired in Chapter Six, who wouldn't let lack of support from her friends deter her from baking her cake? Julia drew the same sort of resolve from her relatives' opposition. The more her family said "No, you can't," the more the little red hen in Julia said "Yes, I can."

Of course, it was her persistence (fueled by her self-belief) that got her through. Yes, she had setbacks initially — she couldn't find the right people to hire, she underestimated her time on jobs in the beginning — but she never gave up. She didn't let worries, fears or negative self-chatter get the better of her. She knew she'd make mistakes. After a while — as we saw in our discussion of Visioncrafting — she welcomed her setbacks, because she learned so much from them. Slowly and steadily, Julia proceeded in her modest but mighty vision quest, not letting disappointments or detractors derail her from the track she'd laid out for herself.

BUMPS IN THE NIGHT

It was only at night, lying awake in bed, that Julia allowed her determination to waver and her self-doubts to loom menacingly in the dark. Her family's attempts to discourage her were one thing, but the inner voices sapping her optimism and questioning her abilities were another matter entirely.

As kids, most of us conjured up imaginary creatures in our bedroom at night, no matter how hard we struggled to fall asleep. As they tucked us in, our parents would tell us to watch out for the bogeyman or not to let the bedbugs bite. Fortunately, we outgrow these fears as we gain control of our lives. But as adults, when we feel unsafe in unfamiliar situations, we go right back to the childhood habit of cringing before our own internal demons. Julia was no exception.

Her personal demons, who turned up the volume on her negative self-chatter while everyone else was sleeping peacefully, sounded something like this:

Who do you think you are?

You're too old.

It's too late.

What a dumb idea.

You've never run a business.

Nobody will want your cleaning services.

You don't have time.

Your family will be angry at you.

When Julia told me about these fears that lurked in the shadow of her nights, I wondered whether she had invested so much energy in shrugging off her family's ridicule that she hadn't taken enough time to listen to and deal with her own doubts. So, together, we went back through the natural progression that she needed to follow to persuade herself that her optimism was well-founded.

In her Visionalysis exercise, I asked Julia to imagine that she had only two minutes left to live. What did she want to do? What would her obituary say? What did Julia want her mourners to say? She knew the answer. Not: "Gee, that was the greatest, most fabulous cleaning service in the world — perfectly operated without a single mistake."

Instead: "That Julia, she went after a second adulthood. She had an idea, she pursued it. Now *that's* an inspiration."

I urged Julia to listen to her fears for a while, not suppress them automatically in her determination to proceed. After all, sometimes fears are realistic appraisals of oneself and one's limits. So she needed to hear them out — just to make sure they were indeed fears and not realistic assessments. And then she learned to argue with them — just as you did in Chapter Five.

Julia knew she was growing older. Instead of defiantly saying, *I'm young enough*, she learned to counter with a positive: *I'm older — but wiser. So I will grow older — while I'm doing something I want to do.*

In the Visioneering phase, Julia went back over the homework she'd done — the discoveries she'd made when she hired other companies and watched them clean. She listened when her friends complained about how hard it was to find good house cleaners — and noted that they all agreed. She reminded herself constantly of the abundant evidence that her idea was good: a top-quality service was needed, and she knew how to make it work.

While Visioncrafting, as she asked the cleaning company workers who came to her house about their businesses, she began to see the companies and their employees as *people* — not gurus, experts, or out-of-this-world talents. In other words, she made them *familiar* so she could begin to envision herself as *one of them.*

Finally, after she began Visionavigating by launching her company, she reminded herself constantly of what she had learned. She repeatedly reassessed her skills and her original idea.

More important, Julia maintained her inspiration when she had setbacks. To do this, she researched people who had embarked on major projects later in life, such as Michelangelo's completion of his *Pietà* sculpture at age ninety — now that was a late-life project if ever there was one. She scrutinized her plan over and over. She became, in her own words, "The Little Engine-vidual Who Could."

JUST SAY YES

In managing relationships with those she loved, she practiced the adage, "First, understand; then, be understood."

This element of Julia's Visionavigating is especially enlightening. Let's look a little closer at what she did.

Her mother had said no. Her grown children had said no. Her sisters had said no. She listened to her mother, sisters, and children — and then she didn't listen to them. After all, they weren't intricately intertwined in her daily life the way her husband John was. So she really listened to him. And he was saying the same thing: no. But Julia listened beyond his words to understand what he really meant:

1. I'm gearing down at work — what am I going to do with that extra time?
2. Travel with me — I've got plans for our life, too.
3. Who will cook my dinner and make me brownies?
4. Don't change. It scares me.
5. Why can't you stay the same person I married?
6. Am I going to be the same person you married, if you become a different person from the one I married?

Get the picture? It's called a natural fear of change. Fear of the unknown. Fear of boat-rocking. Fear of not knowing your lines — or even what play you're in. Julia's husband had the *normal* fears a mate experiences after years of living in a familiar, highly predictable way. After all, he was raised to believe that *he* had the career, and that *his* later-life dreams would be the same as hers.

He wasn't being mean. He didn't love his wife less — he was just scared.

If Julia had not built up so much belief in herself, her husband's fears might have derailed her. If Julia didn't believe her idea was good and possible, then perhaps she would have quit entirely. If Julia had not been persistent, then for sure she would have given in to her husband, and given up on her dream. And if Julia had believed that loving her husband meant she had to abandon her vision, then her plan for a second adulthood would never have come to pass. And her marriage would not have gained in strength and vigor as a result. As you will see, Julia became an admiral of the first rank in the art of Visionavigating.

How did she respond to her husband's concerns?

1. First, and foremost, Julia realized something: Loving her husband did not have to mean the end of loving herself. Let's repeat that in another way: She *could* have her cake and eat it too — if she took the time to understand her husband's fears and address them.

2. She told her husband she wanted to have a great marriage, that she loved him, and that she had a dream that needed his support to help make it happen. She gave him a vital co-starring role, assuring him they would both benefit from her success.

3. She told the truth and promised nothing impossible: She said things would change, that it would be scary at first, but that they would both be better for it later.

4. She reminded him of all the changes they had weathered before: a first child, a second, a third; the death of parents; the flooding of their house; the move to another city. In other words, without their acknowledging it, change had always been part of their lives. And they had been good at it — despite or because of a few ups and downs.

5. She communicated clearly what changes would be necessary: She wouldn't be as available for grocery shopping; She couldn't run some of his errands; they might not be able to go out on both Friday and Saturday nights until she got her work rhythm established. She made it clear what adjustments she expected of him.

6. She thanked him ahead of time for his willingness to experience a little boat-rocking. She reminded him how much it meant to her to have his support. She let him know she knew enough about his own personal background to understand why this might be hard for him.

   John's father had died young. She suspected that John feared the same fate, that he felt he had to cram as much as he could into however many years he had left. Of course, any individual's reasons for harboring fears will vary, but Julia was smart — and loving enough to know some of the private reasons John had.

7. She explained that she was convinced it was important to make this change in her life — even if she didn't know all the reasons.

8. She promised to discuss the business with him and include him in her new work world. She told him his input and support were vital to its success.

Because of her gentle persistence, and her insight into John's emotions, she was able to persuade him that she didn't want to go to her grave playing the IF-ONLY game. To her great joy, he agreed that it was better for her to have had her wish, than wish she had never tried at all.

Buddhism tells us that one of the goals of life is to die while in the process of becoming. Julia embodies this philosophy of continual striving, with her victorious metamorphosis from nurturer to achiever. You can, too.

Here is where your solo journey ends. So far your road map has charted the unknown interiors of your aspirations, the voices within that guide you to your true destination. From here on, the journey is an outward one — into the world of real people, places and things. And you probably won't want to go it alone.

The roads we have taken so far, while uncovering, envisioning, and trying on your dreams, have not required anyone but yourself to keep those dreams on course. You could explore all the possibilities, discover your life's passion, and learn everything you needed to know to pursue it — without involving anyone else unless you chose to.

But if you are to make real-life changes, the support and companionship of those around you is essential. If you have convinced yourself that the only way you can pursue your goals is to sue for divorce or walk out on your family, your assumptions are in for a deafening backfire. Any of your worst nightmares about being alone can come true if you attempt to cut your ties now — and you'll experience a vastly reduced likelihood of succeeding in your new endeavor.

This is not the time to put on your emotional armor and thrash your way to independence. Many women believe the myth that they don't need anybody. I have invariably found this to be a smoke screen to cover up the fear of appearing weak or incompetent in front of those who know us best. Don't take this route: it's a *dead end*. In fact, you'll find it's nigh on impossible even to get out of the parking lot without a little help from your friends.

> *"The fear of being alone becomes a self-fulfilling prophesy . . . . That fear isn't a weakness, to be overcome by toughening up and caring less."*
>
> —BARBARA SHER

I can hear your collective cry: *But how on earth can I get their support? They're not going to like this.* Well, your instincts are probably right: As you begin rolling along toward your new goals, just when you need the most encouragement and support, you *are* likely to get less. Those who are dear to you may object — and not quietly — to the rerouting of the entire family's destinations. After all, they've been used to being driven everywhere *they* want to go, with you in the role of their designated driver. Now, suddenly, the chauffeur has some locations she wants to see.

For a time, this may be the greatest challenge you face: You are navigating through new territory yourself, and you have a car full of passengers telling you which way they want to go. It will be tempting to either give in and continue to take them only to their chosen destinations — or to leave them all at the curb, eating your dust and wondering what on earth has gotten into you.

Neither solution will satisfy you in the long run. Women who dump their personal safety nets wind up agreeing on one thing: When they finally arrive at their goal, they have no one they care about to celebrate with. Though they may be proud of their accomplishments, it's like standing alone at the rim of the Grand Canyon; there's no one to say *"Wow!"* to.

If you can't bring yourself to share your goals with your friends and family because you are absolutely convinced they will sabotage them, ask yourself one last question before shoving your whole plan into reverse and backing up to the status quo: Is giving up on your life's destiny really a disguise for the fear that you will not succeed . . . or the fear that you will lose their love? Remember, women have the right and the resources to be both nurturers and achievers. To deny one side of yourself in deference to the other is to cheat your loved ones out of the opportunity to know and admire the complete person you long to be.

MIND YOUR MESSAGE

How can you recruit your partner's, your parents', and your children's support? And let me remind you, by the way that we're talking about genuine support, not a defensive truce in which communication is resentful and undermining tactics prevail.

First, realize that, deep down, they know it's in their best interests to be part of your team. If your partner has been the only breadwinner for a while, the prospect of change can be enormously intimidating — but he may secretly harbor a longing to be relieved of sole financial responsibility. He may not fully realize this until you bring up your desire to get a job. In fact, he may not realize it for a long time afterward.

On your part, you are probably so unfamiliar with risk and so scared of putting yourself first for a change, that when you communicate your intentions all your fears and anxieties are telegraphed to him. There are always two sides to any relationship. Consider whether his reactions to your new venture stem from the realities of your vision or from the way you're trying to present it to him.

EXERCISE 26: YOU SHOULD HEAR YOURSELF

Let's try something that might help in the delivery of your message. See if you are saying any of the following statements to yourself:

He/she won't let me.

They won't love me if I do what they don't approve of.

I can't do it all by myself.

He/she will stop me.

Look again at the above statements. Do any of them sound familiar? Now write out your own list of reasons involving other people as to why you "can't" move toward your goal. Read them over.

Do you notice that these statements have something in common? They all sound like the statements of a child. Forgive me; I'm not trying to insult you by calling you childish. I'm just asking you to hear the way these statements of helplessness sound to others. Go through them once more; see if you can perceive that for an adult who is free to do whatever he or she chooses responsibly to do, none of these excuses would ring true.

Remember, when you buy into the criticism of those you are close to, you are really saying, "Your approval means everything to me." When you feel guilty or helpless about pursuing your needs, and you allow them to grab the wheel while you take a back seat, you are reverting to the limitations of your childhood.

As a child you did mostly what your parents wanted you to do because you so desperately wanted their love and approval. And besides, the behaviors they requested or demanded of you were essential for your early physical survival. After all, in today's traffic, looking both ways before crossing the street is an essential precaution.

But as you mature, you learn to shed the illusion that your survival hinges on behavior your parents would approve of. Only then can you set your own goals and strive to reach them without fear of placing yourself in real danger. Paradoxically, once you complete the process of growing away from your parents, you can bring more of your true, adult self back into a richer and deeper relationship with them.

As you approach your family with the news of what you have in mind for your own future and theirs, you can expect their reaction to be ambivalent, at best. It helps to understand that their support — while likely to be yours if you will give them time to shift gears — will hardly be yours automatically.

In an ideal world, all love would be unconditional and ever-present. I don't need to tell you that's not how it is. In that same ideal world, everyone would welcome your new aspirations with open arms, be totally flexible, and never interfere with your efforts. We both know this is not true either. People don't like change — theirs or yours.

The fear of change is inherent in most of us; it's one reason your heart beats faster and your pulse quickens just at the thought of pursuing your dream. Fear of change is why others feel threatened or uneasy when you ask them to switch to different routines or different expectations — and especially when you ask them to accept a different version of yourself.

EXERCISE 27: PICKING YOUR TEAM
This exercise can help you define your needs and communicate them with kindness and clarity.

Write down a list of all the people you care a lot about. Put a "C" next to the names of those you think will have to make some Changes when you do. Next, put an "R" next to those from whom you expect Resistance or who will be Resentful of the change. Of these, consider who might try to Undermine your efforts, and put a "U" next to their names.

Finally, who is most flexible and will be most willing to Help you? Put an "H" next to those names. An "H" person might be someone who is close to you, but has little to lose — and perhaps even something to gain — from a radical change in your life. He or she could be a best friend or a sister or coworker who can understand your desires and sympathize with them. When you are looking for the "H" people in your life, concentrate on those who are likely to have your interests at heart and the ability to imagine themselves in your position. Even if they have no particular skills to help your vision process directly, their moral support and availability as sounding boards can be invaluable when you are feeling depleted from dealing with all those "C," "R," and "U" people in your life.

Think long and hard about these people and honestly try to predict their reactions. Keep in mind that they may not fulfill your expectations, but it doesn't hurt to guess.

Now, put aside all of your own dreams and aspirations for the moment, and think about what motivates each of these people. What do *they* like? When do they feel most secure? What lights *their* creative fire? Figure out what each person values, then write this down beside their names. Now look for matches or near-matches between what you need and what they enjoy.

Next comes the greater challenge: Have the courage to put them in charge of whatever part of your dream they seem most eligible to steer. When I say courage, I mean empower them to do their part. It won't be easy, but you must not interfere or boss them about *how* they do it, as long as it gets done. This rare talent — the ability to delegate not only tasks but also authority — characterizes most great leaders. Your goal is to attract investors — not in terms of money, but in terms of energy and commitment — and convince them that they're making an investment in their own satisfaction when they join the team.

> *"I have yet to hear a man ask for advice on how to combine marriage and a career."*
> —GLORIA STEINEM

HEATHER

Heather had always loved art. Every chance she got, she visited museums and shows by local artists; she had even taken a few night courses over the past twenty years. Always in the back of her mind was a wistfulness: *Someday I'd like to do more with my art.*

Married to Joe for thirty years and having raised six children, Heather felt restless. Her two youngest children, aged fifteen and sixteen, were still living at home, and she found herself with more and more free time.

"Joe's really a traditional guy, you know, with the little-woman-in-the-kitchen attitude," she told me. "He'll never be happy if I try to make my hobby into a small business. And, my two kids, I love them dearly, but are you kidding me? They're used to Mom picking up clothes and driving everywhere."

I assured Heather that her possibilities were not as bleak as she felt they were. Yes, many men Joe's age are stuck in outdated thinking about relationship roles and responsibilities. And maybe the kids have gotten away with more than they should have. But approached in an appropriate way, Joe and the teens might even welcome her ideas about branching out on her own. "Really? Do you think so?" said Heather, hardly convinced.

So Heather and I began to work on her feelings of hopelessness about her family's attitudes. First, I asked Heather to make a list of every negative statement she thought Joe or the kids might make if she initiated a change. Here's what her list included:

Why do you feel so restless? Look at all you have to do just looking after us.

I'm sorry, but no wife of mine needs to work.

How much money is it going to cost?

How much time is this going to take?

What most women fear initially when they think of altering the traditional structure of their family life is exactly what Heather was concerned with: discouraging words. Yes, I told Heather; there will be resistance. But if your vision is not cloudy or gray, then you don't have to hear those discouraging words. We needed to do a bit of Visioneering together, to clarify what sorts of art activities Heather wanted to integrate into her life.

I posed the following questions to Heather: What do you really want to do with your art hobby? How many different ways can you apply it to develop a business? Write all of your ideas down. Ask friends, people at art supply and craft stores, museums — anybody you can think of who is involved in that industry who can shed light on how you'll need to prepare yourself. I showed Heather how to Visioneer and suggested she come back to me in a few weeks' time.

After two weeks Heather returned to my office with a giant smile on her face. I hadn't heard such glee and optimism in her voice in months. "I've got it! I'm going to buy posters and frame them. I can sell them to local businesses that are new and need inexpensive, attractive walls. On weekends I can go to local craft shows and sell them there. I can sell them to teenagers. And, even better, I'm going to turn our basement into my workshop so I can be at home. How can they object to that?"

"Heather, that's terrific," I said. "Have you discussed it with your family yet?"

"Well, I mentioned it in passing the other day, just to see any initial reactions they might have. Either everyone is so tuned out they ignore what I say, or they aren't threatened by it. Either way, I don't feel now that it's going to be as hard as I thought to get their cooperation."

Heather's move from helpless–hopeless thinking to feeling more optimistic about her situation enabled her to begin her quest. She was able to turn an avocation into a part-time vocation because she Visioncrafted first to create a plan that could work for her and her family.

Over the course of the eight months Heather and I worked together, she picked a business, crafted it, set up the basement, ordered her business cards, and went to several local craft and art shows. Joe even joins her now on her weekend jaunts to flea markets.

I know that every situation doesn't necessarily work out as smoothly as Heather's did. The important concept to always keep in mind is that the trick of keeping yourself hopeful, optimistic, and realistic creates tremendous momentum. Once you get rolling, you'll soon pick up speed.

Heather was able to defuse her family's fear of change by convincing them that the change would be almost imperceptible, that she would start her business in the family basement and fit it into their preexisting routines. But what if this isn't possible? Sometimes pursuing your dream can mean a radical alteration in your family's lifestyle: you know it and they know it. This is a time when you have no choice but to face your family's fear of change head-on.

This brand of apprehension — a natural response to a sudden and dramatic priority shift on your part — is likely to be displayed by them as anger. But you'll see something interesting going on here: While they are busy being mad, they are also busy making an important distinction. As you direct your energy elsewhere, they have to face up to some new realities.

For instance, maybe you have ceased offering valet service, and you no longer express your love only by doing things for them. Instead they may have to take responsibility for clothes or dishes they use. Don't miss the fact that, sooner or later, they will recognize this shift as a net loss to their comfort. So it isn't that they object so much to what you are going to do for yourself. Instead, they are resisting the thought of what you will no longer be able to do for them.

Meanwhile, you suffer from the fear that if you stop delivering as much in the same way, they'll stop loving you. This fitful stalling of your engine persists when they become resentful and you react by feeling oppressed.

Until you base decisions about your loved ones on values you have established internally, rather than spontaneously as circumstances arise, you will be driving on a collision course without brakes or steering. When you live for others, fulfilling their every need and desire, your relationship eventually accumulates a stockpile of resentment. You will be a much better nurturer when you give from the bounty of your own gratified spirit.

FIND OUT WHAT IT MEANS TO YOU

To gain the respect of others, you must first respect yourself. Acquiring self-respect often involves giving up being too good to others. When you give up over-giving, over-accommodating, you empower yourself. When you introduce your dreams to those you love, their lack of positive response may hurt you deeply. This angst is the high price you have paid for focusing on others at the expense of yourself. You need not make any more payments. This drain on your energies has already cost you too much.

Warn yourself in advance that not everyone around you — not even some of your most loyal friends — will unconditionally support your new quest. Understand that they will see it first from their point of view, not yours. After all, they're only human — which means that you might need to transform yourself, just for a while, into something of a superhuman.

How can you do this? With the help of your old friends who will not let you down: optimism, persistence, and flexibility. Sometimes you need to just keep pressing your foot on the accelerator, because that's what will get you to your destination. Flip your high beams on, look straight ahead, put both hands on the wheel, and tune out all the traffic noise that may surround you.

Once you've managed to hold onto your momentum, you can turn your attention to kindling a fire of enthusiasm among your family and friends. How will you accomplish this superhuman feat? Communication. Talk to them, listen to them, and don't stop trying to help them see your vision from their own perspective.

Even the most tightly woven, loving families probably won't offer the support you need — for the simple reason that they don't know what you need. Because women have traditionally put their own wants second to the wants of those around them, they have few examples to follow, and little skill in communicating what they need. Preparation is the key that opens the door to good communication. Here's an exercise to help you sort out what your own needs are first, and then discover what you may require from others to get these needs met.

EXERCISE 28: WHAT CAN THEY DO FOR YOU?

On a new page of your notebook, write down the items on this list that most apply to your situation:

What I Most Need from Him/Her/Them Checklist:
I wish he/she/they:

____   understood that I am not trying to control or compete.

____   knew I can do it myself.

____   would respect my independence.

____   wouldn't be threatened by my competence or healthiness.

____   knew I want to respect them and have a strong relationship.

____   understood my point of view even if they don't agree with it.

____ understood that support doesn't mean advice — unless I ask for it.

____ would be more cooperative in helping out around the house.

____ would be my friend and want the best for me.

These are only a few of the things you might find important. Take a moment now to add your specific desires to this wish list. Think of as many items as possible.

IT'S HOW YOU SAY IT

How you communicate with your family and friends in presenting your plans for the first time makes an enormous difference to their long-term reaction. Deborah Tannen, in her landmark book on communication differences, *You Just Don't Understand,* says that while men have little trouble communicating facts and tend to use conversation to seek solutions, women speak to share feelings and experiences.

Many other factors influence how we talk to each other, but appreciating what works well is crucial. We express ourselves in a range of ways, from aggressive to passive (and this means nonverbal communication as well). All of us use the entire range, though some of us waste more time in the aggressive end than in the passive end.

Aggressive communication assumes the speaker is superior: *I'm right and you're wrong.* Aggressive expression usually makes the listener defensive — and likely to respond in kind, with as much or even more aggression.

Passive responses, on the other hand, assume an inferiority: *You're right and I'm wrong.* Passive communication often begins with such phrases as, "Well, I'm not sure but . . .," "I may be all wrong, but . . .," or "This may not make any sense, but . . .," Do these sound familiar? When you express yourself passively, frequently you encourage those around you to feel angry and resentful. Passive responses rarely permit a relationship to grow or progress.

In the middle between aggressive and passive lies the most effective, meaningful expression: self-assured. The self-assured woman stands up for her right to express herself — but does not violate others' same rights in the process. She can say no freely, she can state her needs to others, and she doesn't hesitate to disagree — but never resorts to aggression when she does.

Women have traditionally been silent in articulating their beliefs or standing up for their values. The skill of verbalizing their inner desires is one they must take the trouble to learn and then nurture. Are you one of these women? Take this little pop quiz to see how self-assured you are:

1. It's 10 p.m. and your phone rings. Quickly you realize it's a telemarketing call — you know, the kind that starts, "Hello, how are you tonight?" The salesperson launches into a spiel on a product or service you have no interest in. Do you:

   (a) Let the salesperson continue but resolve to stop the next representative who calls from any company.

   (b) Interrupt and politely let the caller know you are not interested.

   (c) Tell the caller to go get a life and hang up.

2. Your partner has recently been pointing out your shortcomings, which serves to undermine your confidence. He's been letting fall derogatory comments, such as "You've never been able to resist that," "You always order the same thing in restaurants," or "You always have to be right." Do you:

   (a) Try to ignore him and hope he will quit, but wonder whether his criticisms are true.

   (b) Tell him you do not appreciate his commenting on your behavior and that it makes you feel attacked. You ask him to stop.

   (c) Retaliate by identifying and making fun of his weaknesses. Or you become sarcastic: "Oh, sure; I really care about what you think."

3. An old friend calls unexpectedly and asks you to meet her for dinner tonight. Do you:

   (a) Change your plans because you don't want to hurt her feelings.

   (b) Tell her that tonight isn't convenient, but with more notice, you'd love to get together.

   (c) Tell her you never can make plans on such short notice and ask her why on earth she thought you'd be free.

Now look back over your answers. If you mostly chose (a), you tend to be passive in the way you react to others. A majority of (b) responses suggests you are more self-assured. Too many (c) responses indicate an aggressive style.

Women are unaccustomed to communicating in a self-assured way. Often, they even question their right to express themselves at all. This questioning leaves them more likely to relate in the manner of either undesirable extreme — aggressively by exploding, or passively by remaining silent or pouting. To evaluate and challenge your own assumptions about your right to vocalize your thoughts and feelings, read over these questions and answer them to yourself:

Should others' needs always come before your own, or are there times when you can put yourself first?

Do you assume that others' opinions are more astute, informed, or well-thought out, and therefore should prevail over yours?

Are you flexible and accommodating to others' views, or do you think it's fairer to compromise to everyone's mutual satisfaction?

Do you feel you have the right to ask for support, or do you think that when you do this you are wasting someone's time?

Do you assume that when someone comes to you for help that you must provide it, or do you feel you have the right to decline taking responsibility for someone else's problem?

The only way to develop a self-assured style of communication is to practice it. Fortunately, since you're Visionavigating at your own personal pace, you can take time to rehearse as much as you want. Before you start, you should be aware of a few basic rules in self-assuredness training. Expressing yourself better involves:

Stating the *facts* as you see them. Be as objective as possible.

Expressing your *thoughts* — that is, how you interpret what the other person says.

Expressing your *feelings*. Only use "I" statements when speaking of emotions, and be specific about how the other person's behavior has made you feel.

Saying what you really *want*.

Here's a sample dialogue to show you how these basic principles work: Nancy is unhappy because her husband Bob acts helpless in the kitchen when she takes classes in the evening. He expects his meals to be prepared in advance so that all he needs to do is microwave them when he gets home from work. He also lets the laundry pile up in the hamper.

NANCY: I'm really tired of having to do everything around here and go to school at the same time (stating the *facts* as she sees them). I think you should be more helpful to me (expressing her *thoughts*). I feel hurt when I think that you don't want to help out (expressing her feelings). I want you to do more for me and yourself around the house when I'm at school or studying (expressing her *wants*).

Now you give it a try. Pick a situation you would like to change. Take a piece of paper and write out your scenario using the above model.

Words can hurt or heal — and it takes very few to do either. Avoiding certain loaded words when you are presenting or negotiating with your support team will help keep the conversation constructive. Two of these loaded words are *always* and *never*. Both tend to make others react defensively because they are absolutes; not too many things in life are always or never true. We resort to these words when we are scared or angry — usually when a conflict has already erupted.

Speaking of conflict, this is inevitable when change is being attempted. The trick is to keep the tension generated by change from turning into open combat, which is counterproductive. To decelerate a disagreement once it is already under way, remember to use "I" statements when describing your feelings, rather than "you" statements. For example: "I don't feel that I'm being heard" is less confrontational than "You never listen to me." Your declarations make assumptions about the other person's motivations and can be heard as accusatory. Restrict your expression to what you truly know — how it feels to be you. Resist the urge to take aim and fire off your opinions about the other person's thoughts and actions.

Another approach that helps to defuse a conflict is changing the discussion to encompass the notion of "we." For instance, when you and your partner have hit a bitter impasse, you could observe, "We seem to be struggling with this topic. Do you have any ideas about why it's so hard for us?"

Even though you may be upset, making the attempt to understand the other person's viewpoint more fully will help you bring your own emotions under control. To do this, summarize what you think the other person has communicated—preferably without judgment— then ask whether your understanding is correct.

When emotions are threatening to become counterproductive, buying time is an acceptable strategy. As long as you aren't agreeing to sweep the problem under a rug forever, you and your partner can benefit from a time-out. If you feel you need to absorb and consider new information presented in the middle of a conflict, you can call a halt and agree to discuss the topic again later. Just make sure you do!

If anger has not threaded its way into your dialogue too deeply, you might try switching sides and arguing the other person's viewpoint. This will not only enlighten you both about each other's priorities, but it might soften a prickly situation with some unexpected humor. Keep all horizons open for a mutually acceptable compromise that leaves both egos intact. If one of you wins and one of you loses, you both lose. Therefore, it is essential that each of you take responsibility for a solution.

> *"No one can make you feel inferior without your consent."*
> —ELEANOR ROOSEVELT

WARNING: CRITICISM AHEAD

Inevitably, as you are tooling along to your goal, someone you respect or love will verbally sideswipe you. With practice, you can become adept at taking criticism the same way you handle setbacks and mistakes. It isn't the nature of the comment (or the nature of your mistake) that matters; it's how you choose to think about it. Like making a mistake, receiving negative feedback doesn't have to be uncomfortable or unproductive. It can be seen as yet another opportunity to learn. After all, the feedback of others can be accurate. If your reaction is always defensive, you will miss out on useful opportunities to progress and improve.

But how do you tell whether the critique is valid? When you are criticized, ask yourself the following questions. Keep in mind that no one but you can be the judge and jury for your internal convictions:

Is the censure based in fact or is it merely the person's conclusions or opinion?

Is this the first time I've heard this criticism?

Does the criticism seem logical?

Does the person criticizing me have credentials (experience, education, background) I respect?

Did anything unusual prompt this person to offer the criticism?

Is there someone else who can confirm or dispute this claim?

Does the criticism relate to something I care about, or is it irrelevant to achieving my goal?

Does the criticism relate to something I can change or want to change?

How would someone I admire have responded to this criticism?

You may end up with a hung jury—agreeing to disagree with your detractors. You can validate their right to offer an opinion by saying that you can see why they drew such a conclusion and telling them why you disagree. Thank the critic and enlist his help if possible. I guarantee that you'll feel much better than you would if you'd simply gone off to lick your wounds in private. Taking some time to analyze the actual nature of the criticism, to examine the motives of the critic, and to sort out what verdict your internal court delivers is an important part of Visionavigating. If you don't do it now, you're very likely to run into the very same criticisms, somewhere down the road.

> *"Rejection is just one person's opinion. You cannot take it personally, or it will destroy your confidence and keep you from moving on."*
> —BARRY J. FARBER, AFTER TWENTY-SIX REJECTIONS OF HIS BEST-SELLING BOOK, *BREAKTHROUGH SELLING*

HAVING TO SAY YOU'RE SORRY

Too often, you can get stuck at a green light and start spinning your tires because you fear that gaining ground in your quest means losing ground in the relationship. In your desperation to get under way, you can easily wind up doing and saying things you might regret later.

That's okay; we all miscommunicate sometimes. This is a detour that you can recover from.

Just remember the power of a sincere apology. A simple, heartfelt "I'm sorry" does not mean that you're conceding. In fact, it's a sign of strength, not weakness. You are letting the other person know how much the relationship matters to you.

Of course, your aim is to convince your friends and family of the value of your quest without having anything to apologize for. To improve your chances of never having to say you're sorry, remember that the initial manner in which you present your master plan makes an enormous difference in how well it is received.

Let's say you have already spent nine months of effort in Visionalysis, Visioneering, and Visioncrafting. A combined interest in teaching and computers led you to the discovery that you want to become a personal computer coach. You've gathered everything you need to know before getting started. Now you're ready to present this fait accompli to your family. Here's an important hint: Don't start by saying you have it all worked out, even if you do! Don't assure them you won't need any involvement on their part, just their cooperation and assistance with household chores. Is this any way to recruit a team?

Instead, tell them you have an idea that you'd like their opinion about. The difference between "Here's what I'm going to do" and "Tell me what you think of this idea" is the difference between a closed door and an open one.

Once you have their receptive attention, go on to engage them in your adventure. Share with them your highest hopes — along with your darkest fears of failure. Don't point to all the work you have already done. Instead, emphasize all the things you still have to do. Now you've given them room to like certain aspects of your plan and make suggestions regarding the parts they don't like. They can offer support or other perspectives on the validity of your fears.

Let them in on your dream. Don't be defensive. Never fall into the trap of thinking you have to present a totally confident front. It's okay to show some fear and vulnerability. Once you have issued this open invitation to become involved, they will love offering their suggestions and may even follow up with practical help.

Sharing your hopes with others in an honest, open fashion will do wonders for your outlook as well. When you explain your concerns to your family it might well be the very first time you have voiced these trepidations out loud. You'll be surprised at how much more manageable they will seem than when they were just rattling around in your head! Your loved ones may have good ideas on how to minimize your obstacles. If not, at least you mentioned them first, before they got a chance to point them out to you.

It can be heartening to watch your friends and family rally to your cause when they see a supporting role for themselves in it. Adults may become surprisingly brotherly, sisterly, or parental, offering that familial warmth that is so helpful in a new endeavor. And never underestimate the creativity of children in problem-solving. What adults spend hours hassling over, a child may glance at and ask, "Why don't you do it this way?" and leave you awestruck at your own lack of insight.

At first you may think it silly or awkward to prepare a formal presentation for someone you might see every day at the breakfast table. But no matter how you have to do it — the easy way or the hard way — you will discover that such preparation is vital.

The best way to get yourself ready to present your ideas to the people who matter most in your life is to prepare a personal script. This will give you a version of your dream that you can return to when their inevitable interruptions and exclamations put you in danger of wandering off course. Here are some thoughts to help you in preparing your script:

Be positive. Say: "I know you want to see me achieve my goals," rather than: "I don't know if you realize how important this is to me."

Don't apologize by going on about how you know this is going to upset their schedule; don't say, "I'm sorry to be asking for this, but . . . ."

Write down all the points you want to make, everything they will need to know if they're going to buy into your dream. Avoid directives designed to change them or their attitudes; only they can accomplish that. Overconfident assumptions, such as, "I think you're really going to like this," can often bring on the exact opposite reaction.

For now, avoid being specific about how many hours, which days, which tasks. Remember, this is all new to them; they will feel excluded and trapped — and see more negatives — if you dictate exactly what changes they need to make.

Communicate your certainty by demonstrating that this is a no-looking-back change. Don't demand their support. Suggest that your new venture has a much better chance of succeeding with their support. Avoid using the word "need" in reference to their role, because it implies you can't do it unless they comply. This will make them feel trapped — or, worse, will show them a way that they can trap you. Let them know you value their potential contribution because you realize it can be done better together than alone. Request that they think and talk about what they each can do to move your idea forward. Help them help you: Ask what they think you might do next in pursuit of your goal.

If their immediate reaction to any new adjustments is negative, you must stay positive. Remind them of all the other adjustments you, as a couple or a family, have already made — like when you found out that twins were on the way instead of one baby. Or when the cellar flooded and you had to live with relatives until it could be cleaned and repaired. Or when one of you came home with the bad news that you had been laid off from your job. Remember how Julia reminded her husband of all the challenges they had met together?

Prepare for the discouragement viruses they will try to infect you with. Before going to the meeting, inoculate yourself against such an invasion by rehearsing what you might say in response. Making a list of similar obstacles you have already overcome as a family will prompt you to bring them up when family members resist.

Avoid using "you" or assigning feelings, like "I know you may find this difficult . . ." or "I know you are not going to like this, but . . . ." No one appreciates being told ahead of time how they will feel. You are signaling that you expect trouble — and certainly increasing the odds that you will get it.

If a family member or friend responds negatively or with sarcasm, confront them in an understanding and reassuring way. Using the word *and* instead of *but* will help immeasurably with this. For instance, instead of

> "I know this is an adjustment *but* I don't think it is going to be as bad as you think" or

> "I know this is a change *but* I'd like you to help me with it;"

You can be much more convincing when you opt for alternatives employing *and*:

> "I know this is an adjustment *and* I don't think it is going to be as bad as you think" or

"I know this is a change *and* I'd like you to help me with it."

You may be thinking, *How am I going to remember all this when the time comes?* Do you think moderators or luncheon speakers remember everything they have to say? Do what they do — write out your responses ahead of time on index cards. Carry them in your purse and in spare moments — perhaps when you are waiting at a real red light — take them out and practice, practice, practice. Once you have a script you are satisfied with, try it out on a trusted friend — preferably one who knows your audience as well. This feedback can further polish your presentation.

While we're on the subject of getting help from others, it's a good idea to have somebody you can consult throughout the many phases of your pursuit. It should be someone who unquestionably cares about you and has your best interests at heart. This person might be a colleague who is attempting something similar, or a mentor who is already doing something like your vision. Maybe as a child you learned to swim using the buddy system. It's reassuring to have someone keeping tabs on your whereabouts, especially when you encounter deep waters of resistance that threaten to drown you.

But don't expect your buddy to tell you or your loved ones what to do. After all, that's what so much of this journey is about: getting rid of backseat drivers and inner voices from your past. When you ask for and take the exact advice of others too frequently, you prevent yourself from building up your own sense of mastery. Gathering information from others and getting their opinions is one thing; looking to them for answers on which way to turn at intersections usurps your role as the driver of your dream.

Here's some food for thought: When you tell your immediate family about your new venture, you'll need to be mentally sharp, well-rested — and well-fed! Few people appreciate the vital role that nutrition plays in maximizing brain function during stressful moments. First, don't eat heavily — even if this is one of your sources of comfort — when you are planning to present your idea. A large meal brings more blood to your digestive tract, which deprives your brain. To stay mentally sharp, eat protein and avoid carbohydrate-rich foods like pasta, rice, and potatoes. Protein alone tends to stimulate brain power; try fish or a lean cut of meat. Refuse drinks with sugar (a carbohydrate). And remember those foods high in flavonoids that can even reduce stress — onions, apples, tea, and grapes.

I strongly recommend that you gather the family together for a formal powwow. The purpose of this meeting is to begin defining what the needs and priorities are for everyone in the family — not just you. Giving each member a voice helps get cooperation by making them feel heard, not discounted. You will encounter less resistance because they will feel like partners in the new venture.

Now that you are ready, pick a time that gives you maximum chance for positive reactions. This does not mean Saturday morning if everyone has plans for the day, or 10 p.m. on a Thursday when you are all tired and ready for bed. You might try letting them pick a time: Empower them and set their curiosity spinning by asking when they can spare an hour to talk about something new.

Because I have recommended that you prepare carefully for this presentation, and I've gone on to say that timing is critical, you may have the impression that what you are giving is a sales pitch, and that your fate lies in the balance depending on whether they "buy" your proposal. Keep in mind — even as you begin your discussion with them — that you are eventually going to enlist their cooperation in pursuing this vision regardless of their initial response. This will help you explain your intentions without the appearance of seeking permission or selling them on the idea. Convey to them that they are vital to this venture — but that the direction it takes will be yours to decide.

> *"Getting good players is easy — it's getting them to play together that's the hard part."*
> —CASEY STENGEL

chapter 12

Backseat Drivers

I wish I could promise that you'll have unconditional support in your newfound endeavor. But you know better, don't you? Naysayers abound; you can always find someone who will give you advice based on their own fears: colleagues who envy you, parents who pictured you doing something else, friends who seem to want to infect you with their fears.

Make it a habit never to ask others, "Can I?" They tend to answer for themselves, not for you. Don't give up that power to decide whether you can or not. In fact, don't even ask yourself if you can. Ask, instead, *HOW can I do it?* I'm not saying you should be blind to your own weaknesses. In fact, one of the best ways to know how *not* to go about achieving your goal is to acknowledge your own limitations.

But to ignore naysayers, you first have to maintain belief in yourself. This sometimes involves practicing some selective hearing. Let me explain.

At this point, you may be thinking, *It's not worth the turmoil it will produce in my mate. He's not going to like this.* Your suspicions are probably right on the money. It has been my experience that the person most likely to resist change in your life will be your partner. Although we are deeply hurt by their lack of support, it is not at all unusual.

Mates perceive your change as unwanted and unnecessary boat-rocking. They are convinced the boat will capsize if they don't take the helm. They're scared they will lose, not gain, as you grow. This fear can be expressed in as many ways as there are mates, but one common pattern of behavior is what psychologists call passive-aggressive.

Here is an example: Mike knew that Cheryl had to be at her computer class at 4 p.m. After much negotiation, he agreed to pick up the kids at school. One day Cheryl got beeped fifteen minutes after she sat down in class. The kids were waiting alone outside in freezing weather. When confronted with what happened, Mike simply said, "I forgot."

Certainly we all forget things. But what you need to know is that Mike had fought Cheryl's returning to school. He didn't like the fact that she would be less available at home, and that if she went on to graduate she would be on an equal educational footing with him. He was challenged by this, and didn't know how to express it. His anguish took the form of "forgetting" to do something he saw as her proper duty.

Here is a list of other possible passive-aggressive behaviors you are likely to encounter. Check off the ones you have seen or expect to experience.

___ Procrastinating

___ Backstabbing

___ Being chronically late or absent

___ Sending mixed messages

___ Acting helpless

___ Giving you subtle personal put-downs

___ Saying disparaging things to the kids behind your back

___ Withdrawing

___ Not suggesting solutions

___ Not going out of his way

Passive-aggressive behavior represents the classic double bind: Your partner giveth with one hand and taketh away with the other. What you are left with is the no-win feeling, *I'm damned if I do and damned if I don't.*

Sometimes the best way out of this bind is to negotiate honestly. By declaring yourself willing to discuss the conflict, you hand your partner the power to stop acting out in a passive-aggressive manner. A negotiator for professional athletes' endorsement contracts recommends doing an honest assessment of how much leverage you have: Are you indispensable or difficult to replace in your family? Probably so.

Remember the story of the three little pigs and the big bad wolf? The wolf comes to the door disguised in sheep's clothing. But the pigs aren't fooled. The big bad wolf huffs and puffs but can't blow the brick house down. Likewise, your family may huff and puff, but your well-built plans will not succumb to their intimidation. Stick to your guns. It might help to imagine yourself in a house: They are outside trying to knock it down. See yourself inside, calmly holding down the fort.

Often, your mate's underlying, unspoken fear is that you will not need him as much if you become more independent. If you don't need him as much, you could possibly leave. Abandonment is most human beings' greatest fear, so don't underestimate its power. He does not realize that departure is not what you intend at all — that you seek a closer, stronger bond, based on mutual growth and sharing.

Paradoxically — as you learned in your Visionalysis — we often create exactly what we fear. So if he fears abandonment, he will act in a way that forces you away. He may try to reinstate his control by being possessive or cross-examining your every move, or he might withdraw and become uncommunicative. Either way, he loses. And so, of course, do you.

Some psychologists and therapists advocate dealing with manipulative or sabotaging partners by just saying, "Tough. I'm going to do it anyway regardless of how you feel." But I suggest you have more to gain from an empathetic, balanced approach. Attempt to find out what your life partner is afraid of, and then ask him to make some suggestions about how the two of you might be able to cooperate better.

Rest assured, I understand it is not easy to rock the boat and change long-standing relationship patterns. But it is essential to do this if you are going to grow and realize your vision. Try to rock it gently at first. And if that doesn't work, rock harder! We all want to believe that those we love want only the best for us. Unfortunately, because they may be insecure, those who are supposed to love us most don't always act in our best interests, or their own, even though they may really want to.

Here are some things to consider if you conclude that rocking the boat is not worth the waves it will create in your most valued relationship. Are *you* being paralyzed by a fear of abandonment? Are you afraid your partner will leave you if you persist in pursuing this change? Are you afraid you won't be loved? Do you think that after coming this far — discovering and planning how to go after your dream — that you will forget it all, and go back to the way things were? Do you think that you can resist becoming resentful that you have not had the chance to grow, the chance to find out if you could have done it? Do you see that it is likely that the relationship — sooner or later — will become stressed anyway?

> *"If you always do what you always did, you will always get what you always got."*
> —Source Unknown

FACE THEIR FEARS

When you make the assumption that your partner or loved ones are not going to like what you have in mind, you are not giving them the chance to think for themselves. Maybe they will overreact to the initial prospect of a change. But will they actually dislike the positive changes in you? Does your partner usually want what is best for you? Remember, most relationships thrive when both people are growing mentally and have independent aspirations. In the best of partnerships, neither party is weak, needy, or helpless without the other. Both parties cooperate and support one another.

One way to spot the insecurities of those around you is to listen closely to their opinions of other women who have followed and achieved their dreams. If your close friends or family put down the choices of successful women they don't know, chances are they will think similarly about your departure from the expected path and schedule.

People outside your family can also become quite upset when challenged by your branching out. For example, if you decide to get a job, other mothers in your neighborhood, church, synagogue, or community group may feel threatened by your leaving the caravan and pulling out into the passing lane. Some may simply be convinced that your place, like theirs, is in the home. Others may be afraid their husbands might say to them, "If she can do it, why can't you?"

You may even feel guilty about creating distance between yourself and these friends or relatives. When their more narrow horizons cannot encompass your aspirations, you blame yourself for outgrowing them. Or when your family members, reflecting their own limitations, voice their doubts about your abilities, you feel disloyal because you disagree with their opinions.

I repeat: You do not have to lose these people from your life if you take the time to understand yourself and them. Make sure you have explained what you want clearly; your clarity helps dispel their doubts and concerns. Avoid shaming or blaming; instead, face your fears, and theirs, openly.

Sometimes, however, when the going gets tough and the road seems impassable, you should give yourself and them a break. Just pull into the first available rest stop. Prolonged exposure to their exhaust can be hazardous to your confidence and ambition. At least for a while, reducing time spent talking to them about your goals is advisable. You can always resume your trip from the last exit, or find a detour around their objections.

Children can be as needy as spouses — maybe even more so. They can be sullen and rebellious at the idea of change. They can try to make you feel guilty — and, boy, are they good at it! Some children are more flexible than others, but they will still grow resentful if they feel they've been left out of the decision making.

Most kids are adept at manipulation and are great guilt-inducers. After all, their survival may depend on it. They will often pout, or illogically blame some bad occurrence or feeling on your new venture. On the bright side, however, when they discover they are proud of what you are trying to accomplish, or are enjoying their role in your enterprise, children's enthusiasm helps them to better support your efforts. Reward this!

Parents, who have known you the longest, may find your shift in identity even more difficult to accept. They often disguise discouraging remarks as attempts to be protective: "Are you sure you have the time? You seem so busy already." "Think it over carefully; are you sure you're not taking on too much?" Or even this confidence demolisher: "You seem so self-centered; we feel as if we hardly know you."

Many parent-child relationships, for a variety of reasons, never make the transition to an adult–adult exchange. Parents continue to over-advise rather than respect their children as trustworthy grown-ups. And you may have played a willing role in keeping that collusion alive — until now.

As an adult, it's time for you to point out when your parents are being unnecessarily critical. They are trying to push their views, emphasize their needs for you; so tell them that you need their support, not their put-downs. Keep in mind the motives behind their comments and actions: They are defending their own beliefs. It will help you — and minimize your own defensiveness — just to be aware of what they are experiencing.

One strategy that can short-circuit your parents' or childrens' opposition is to adopt a technique from the martial art of Aikido. In practice, this means turning the force of an opponent's resistance against him or her — making their strength work for you. When your teenage son comes up with ten reasons why your going back to college is a goofy idea, point out that because you will need to study in your free time, the car will be more available for his use. Aikido means responding to opposition in a surprising and clever way — without aggression. Without lecturing, you have planted the seed that this change is not win–lose, but win–win.

Other people may try to undermine your confidence and sabotage your efforts, even when they are not directly involved in your life. Friends of your immediate family, or in-laws, including brothers- and sisters-in-law, fall into this category. In the movie *The Godfather*, when Don Corleone passes the reins of power to his son Michael, he advises, "Keep your friends close, but keep your enemies closer."

I think Don Corleone means that, instead of bristling or becoming defensive, it's wiser to be nice to those you suspect don't necessarily have your best interests at heart. Instead of telling them to mind their own business, you can court their interest. This encourages them to trust and cooperate with you so you can, at all times, be aware of their motives. That's one secret of staying in power and control of your destiny.

Both Hands on the Wheel

You must prepare yourself for the winds that will blow you from one side of the road to the other. This will be a time of upset and disequilibrium. It will take tremendous courage, fortitude, and focus to keep driving forward as some of the people you love resist.

At this crucial juncture, do not lose your cool. Be calm and do not overcorrect if you go into a skid. Don't jerk the wheel in the opposite direction or hit the brakes hard; that's what your detractors want you to do. I know it's not easy. Your natural inclination will be to feel totally out of control, overwhelmed with anxiety; you will want to reverse course and speed back to the safety of where you started out. Sometimes it helps to remind yourself that this supreme effort — getting the meaningful people in your life to cooperate in helping you achieve your goals — is merely stressful, not life-threatening. You're not going to die trying.

One successful entrepreneur is fond of telling her employees, "If it's not nuclear war, we can handle it." This philosophy helps her, and them, keep their challenges in perspective. The point is to get your family and friends to see your point of view and feel safe riding in your Visionmobile.

It's in your interest to go ahead and describe your aspirations to the best of your ability, then explain the changes that need to take place. Spell out what you are asking them to do to help you (notice I did not say "let" you or "enable" you). Now give them the right not to like it.

The significant people in your life may display a rainbow of emotions from glad or sad to ticked off. Let them whine and complain and moan and groan if they like. Let them give you the silent treatment and pout. That's okay. Instead of defending your decision, give them some time to absorb the idea.

One option women usually won't consider is to *let them be mad.* You're not a child anymore. You need not fear your parents' umbrage as you did when you were very small. In fact, you're looking out for their welfare when you allow them time and space to be angry about the change. Because they are not your parents, you don't need their permission — so don't seek it. If you have to, consider the possibility that you can pursue your goal without their unconditional approval.

High achievers have a well-kept secret: They do not enjoy 100 percent support from their entire family — or even employees and colleagues — all the time. One skill they practice is not taking others' responses personally. Although being sensitive to people's feelings about you is important, avoid relinquishing the power to judge you to anyone else. This is *your* job.

> *"The way I see it, if you want the rainbow,*
> *you gotta put up with the rain."*
> —Dolly Parton

DON'T GET MAD, GET GOING

Enough about their needs, for just a moment. What about your own anger? "After all I've done for them ..." is a common, often well-founded response to resistance from family members. Remember, anger is a seductive emotion. It's energizing — even exhilarating. But the notion that expressing anger is the best way to get rid of it is a destructive fallacy. Expressing rage merely stimulates the brain, making you feel more angry, not less. Your best strategy is neither to suppress nor vent your anger, but simply to acknowledge it privately. Recognize when you feel angry. Take note of it. This separates you from its source and gets you focusing on your body instead of your mind. Notice when your heart or temples begin to pound, when you feel hot, when you clench your jaw or grind your teeth in frustration. Then concentrate on relaxing your jaw, ceasing the grinding, letting your shoulders drop. Take a deep breath, exhale slowly, and relax.

Resistance must be met with an artful blend of your emotions, which means you have to keep them under control. You'll need two parts defiance — an internal "just watch me" attitude in which you let adversity light a fire under you; and one part patience — the perception that resistance is simply a problem to be solved, not a parking brake that is stuck forever. You may even recognize in these traits your old fellow travelers, optimism and persistence.

In the midst of all your loved ones' objections, your conviction will be tested to the maximum. If you find yourself wavering, reach back to the exercises you performed while gathering strength for your quest, and run through them again. The minute you stop believing you can do it, your momentum will screech to a halt and stall out — probably in the middle of a busy intersection.

You're Visionavigating now; this is for real. When you're out there on the road, you must learn to depersonalize roadblocks. Make informed choices that are indisputably *your* choices. To have conviction, you must act with conviction. This will help keep all your backseat passengers calm, well-behaved, and confident that you know what you're doing.

Remember, even if both you and your loved ones experience some anger, you are creating a new language within your family. Eventually, all members will possess the vocabulary to express and chase their individual dreams in a shared journey. Through team effort and support, not just your goals but all family members' dreams can be realized.

Somewhere along this fascinating family trip, you may be surprised to learn that your family doesn't judge or love you just for the things you do or the role you play — but for who you really are. Toss your old role-playing habits out the window — never to be seen again.

BUILDING A BETTER FAMILY

Team effort and support sounds enticing, doesn't it? It's not only a means to facilitate your achievement; it's a marvelous achievement all its own. But to accomplish this, you must introduce empathy, flexibility, and understanding into your family communication network. Getting everyone on the same wavelength is the key.

Creating a *shared mental model* with your family members will allow you to understand their fears, and — most importantly — help them help you. Even if you don't understand their fears and needs completely, a shared mental model creates a team and demonstrates that you will take into consideration their requests, needs, and fears. Using the mental model helps develop compassion, cooperation, and solution-based approaches.

In a true team effort, everyone's input is heard and considered. The goal is to develop adaptability using each other's strengths — not exploiting anyone's weaknesses. When individuals in a couple or family share a mental model, they grow closer by working as a team to help each other. Here's an example of how you can build one wing of a shared mental model.

Almost without exception, if you are going to divert some energy elsewhere, the people you are living with will have to pitch in on daily household chores. They may valiantly promise to do so, but in all likelihood will develop instant amnesia and will not fulfill their obligations.

This puts you in the impossible role of superwoman. Not only are you committed to achieving your personal dreams, but now you must continue to be a full-time wife, full-time mom, full-time daughter.

Unfortunately, "full-time" means just what it says. You can't be full-time at more than one job. Something will eventually give, and it's likely to be you — unleashing all that guilt you feel about putting yourself first for a change. The most tempting choice will be to abandon your goal and return to old habits. You don't want to do this, do you? So you'll have to construct a shared mental model, so that all family members can see where they fit into the challenge of running the household. It's time for a chore chat.

To negotiate a new regime for accomplishing the family chores, call another family powwow. Try establishing a routine with the following considerations:

1. Make a list of chores necessary for the entire family to function each day (feed the dog, make breakfast), each week (replace kitty litter, grocery shop), and each month (put the recycling out on the right day).

2. Define each job in its entirety — nitpicking if you must — so that everyone agrees what satisfactory completion means: If you empty the kitchen trash, you also replace the plastic liner with a fresh one.

3. Allow each person to pick one chore, then do rounds until all are assigned. This allows everyone to have choices and avoidances — and to feel they have participated in the decisions.

4. Who are the police who will make sure everything gets done? I'm joking. Optimally, no one has to do any policing. If someone can't complete a chore, you discuss it, you negotiate a trade for another chore, or you compromise if a child finds a chore too difficult.

5. Periodically monitor, review, and revise the list and the details describing each task. Have an abbreviated chore chat to let everyone in on any new chores (sweep leaves off the new satellite dish) and any redefinitions of old chores (cleaning the bathroom does *not* mean throwing all your sister's cosmetics in the trash). At this session, let members trade tasks to relieve boredom and cross-train. Or do another complete selection round.

Using these more unifying techniques can transform chores from moans and groans into life lessons in negotiation and cooperation for everyone involved.

Goals, once they're identified and the route is mapped out for their achievement, conform to a kind of cruise control. If you slow down or stop, they have a funny way of tailgating you until you reaccelerate. At this critical point, it is important to keep your hands firmly on the steering wheel and your foot on the accelerator.

You have to learn sometime that you are loved for just being you — not for how many errands you do, meals you cook, or clothes you wash — and now is as good a time as any. This may require living with some internal guilt and fear. Understand that you are making a shift to practicing some self-care habits. No longer the passive receiver of whatever appreciation happened to come your way, you are now the active producer of your own sense of accomplishment.

If you want to keep going and going and going toward your dream like the Energizer Bunny, it's up to you to keep your internal batteries charged. Without becoming obsessed with achieving your goal, shift out of neutral. Then, gear by gear, work up to the speed you enjoy, traveling in the direction you have chosen.

Here is a checklist of hints for keeping yourself fully charged in your Visionavigation:

____ Make time for yourself.

____ Make time for your family.

____ Make time for friends.

____ Surround yourself with the most positive, optimistic people you can find.

____ Be open to new avenues, even other means of getting to the same place.

____ Know what you don't know — and when to ask for help.

____ Convince yourself that you have every right to be chasing your dream — that regardless of your inexperience, you are a player.

____ Don't try to do it all — delegate.

____ Don't say yes just because someone asks you to do something.

____ Let your support team take part in your decisions.

____ Take small steps so your support team can adjust at their own pace.

____ Let new technologies be the oil in your engine — easing, expediting, relieving you and your support team of tasks.

____ When you need help or encouragement, call on family and friends.

____ When you have a small success, or complete one step toward your goal, invite those who have supported you to celebrate.

_____   Laugh! At each crisis. At the bigger problem you created trying to solve a little one. At your mistakes. At yourself.
Laughter is not only a stress reliever, it's a battery charger; it
gives you the energy and commitment to keep going.

GRETA

Greta wanted to move out of her big house in the suburbs. She wanted
to write a new lease on life by returning to a city apartment — like the
one she had grown up in years before. Married twenty-two years to
Marv, and with a daughter now eighteen and ready to leave for college,
Greta feared that her family would think she was nuts: Move to the city
with all its traffic and crime? Why?

Greta finally called the family together. The focus of the powwow
was to address the following issues:

1. What features do each of us need in a home and neighborhood
   (how much room, convenience to stores, work)?
2. What will be most difficult to give up (familiar house, friends,
   memories, space, privacy)?
3. What are our "must-haves" (convenient parking, reasonable
   commute to work or school, safe neighborhood)?
4. What shared goals do we have (simpler lifestyle, less
   maintenance)?
5. What is each member of the family willing to sacrifice or toler-
   ate (being neater in more confining space, putting up with more
   noise and closer neighbors)?
6. What is each person afraid will happen if they move to the city
   (muggings, loss of friends or privacy)?

Greta presented her goal as an idea to explore together, not as a
done deal. And she shared her doubts and worries along with her
hopes. She let her family provide their input, so they felt the decision
was coming from them too. Then all participants got at least a part of
what they wanted. This created a win-win situation for Greta's family.

If you expect intense opposition to your idea, one technique I find
useful when you meet resistance is to *agree*. You actually agree with the
other person's statement and then interject your reply. For instance,
when Marv said, "I'm not going to give up my garden," Greta's reply
could have been: "You know, Marv, you're right. It isn't going to be the

same. And I know this will seem like a big sacrifice. I'll certainly need your help finding an apartment with a roof deck where you can still grow your tomatoes."

Don't hesitate to role-play this technique in your imagination and get used to using it appropriately. This is another time when writing out possible dialogues on index cards and practicing them can help you get ready. When you are prepared, you can shrug off your own defensive reaction and develop a thick skin — without seeming unsympathetic to the needs of your loved ones.

I sincerely hope that as your new routine begins to become familiar and your family stops grumbling about new responsibilities, one fine day will arrive when someone sheepishly confesses that it is more fun than they thought it would be. Or you might overhear one of them bragging about your new role to a friend. Or they may even tell you they're proud to be part of your effort.

What a great gift you will have bestowed on your loved ones: the opportunity to feel a helpful, necessary, and indispensable part of your fully realized vision. In the final analysis, your family wants most to be loved, and included — invested in your dream. Strive to forge — from what may have been a loose and uncomfortable knot — a tight and loving bond in the relationships that matter to you most.

SUMMARY: VISIONAVIGATING

1. Don't try to go it alone, without the support of the people who matter to you most. If you do succeed in reaching your goal without them, you'll find that it can be very lonely at the finish line.
2. Mind your message. Consider whether your loved ones are reacting to your vision, or to the way that you convey it. Are you conveying your fears and anxieties to them?
3. Make allowances for others' resistance to a change in you, and carefully pick a team of supporters according to their ability to accept and invest in your dream.
4. Remaining hopeful, optimistic, and realistic creates the momentum you'll need to override others' fear of change.
5. Take time to develop a self-assured style of communicating your thoughts and feelings, and handling the conflicts or criticisms that may arise.

6. Understand and empathize with your loved ones' fears — but don't give in to them. You don't need their permission, so don't seek it.

7. Don't give in to anger, either. Keep your eyes on the road instead, and keep moving.

8. Create a shared mental model of your new life, so that you and your family know what to expect from each other.

9. Remember that Visionavigating takes time and timing, patience and persistance. Even when you stop moving forward, find ways to keep the dream engine revving.

10. Acknowledge the spiritual and communal aspects of your personal vision, and consider their important roles in the rest of your life.

11. Celebrate your quest as it progresses, and savor the good influence that your brave new pursuit will have on your sons and daughters, and all who come after you.

chapter 13

The Long and Winding Road

"Real isn't how you are made," said the Skin Horse. "It's a thing that happens to you. When a child loves you for a long, long time, not just to play with, but really loves you, then you become Real."

"Does it hurt?" asked the Rabbit.

"Sometimes," said the Skin Horse, for he was always truthful. "When you are Real you don't mind being hurt."

"Does it happen all at once, like being wound up," he asked, "or bit by bit?"

"It doesn't happen all at once," said the Skin Horse. "You become. It takes a long time. That's why it doesn't often happen to people who break easily, or have sharp edges, or have to be carefully kept. Generally, by the time you are Real, most of your hair has been loved off, and your eyes drop out and you get loose in the joints and very shabby. But these things don't matter at all, because once you are Real you can't be ugly, except to people who don't understand."

—From Margery Williams,
The Velveteen Rabbit

The Skin Horse's depiction of what it means — and what it takes — to be Real strikes a chord in the hearts of those people who have dared to ask for more from their lives, and from themselves. What begins as a vague restlessness, a sense of something missing or left behind, can evolve into the sort of heart-stirring quest that transforms an ordinary life into a pageant of grace and passion.

In these pages you have read about women — Annie, Carol, Libby, Sook, Julia, and the rest — who went from *wanting* something more to *being* something more. And perhaps you have discovered in yourself the wellspring of optimism and persistence that will enable you to mirror their success — in your own way, as a reflection of your unique vision.

If you remain unsure of where that tantalizing vision will lead you, and you still see too many red lights in front of you, don't be disappointed. This process takes time. And it also takes timing. As long as you refuse to abandon your quest, and continue to take whatever actions you can to keep it alive, I promise that someday the road ahead will open up for you, beckoning you to drive to your dream.

In the meantime, don't let yourself idle helplessly. You've already displayed the initiative you needed to read this book and complete the exercises, so you know you have what it takes to navigate your vision when the time is right. For now, I ask you to put this book down for about two weeks. At the end of that period, pick it up again, along with your notebook, and go back over the answers you wrote to yourself. I wouldn't be surprised if some new patterns emerge for you at this point.

Another tactic you can try, especially if you are a "people person" who is stimulated into action by the encouragement of those around you, is to form a Green Light Study Group. You probably know other women who, like you, want to explore their own possibilities. You can share ideas, even exchange your exercises with one another, and discuss aspects of your vision process. And your wanderings don't need to stop with the pages of this book. In the back you'll find a list of resources and further readings; I've compiled this as a departure point for you to continue your progress without me.

No journey is ever complete. As you have probably figured out by now, Visionavigating is more of a beginning than an end. In that sense, this book doesn't really have an ending — unless you count the one that will be filled in, someday, by you.

So, wherever you are on the road, remember that nurturing and achieving are different paths to the same end. And consider the possibility that you are much farther along than it may seem. By reading this book, doing some of the exercises, and giving serious thought to your ultimate destination, you've already traveled much nearer to the essential mysteries of life than most people.

Before I leave you to pursue your vision, fueled by all the new knowledge that you've gained by seeing your own future and steering bravely toward it, I want to discuss some end-of-life issues: retirement, spiritual fulfillment, and celebration of the journey itself. I think you'll see that, as a woman already in touch with her genuine desires, you're well on your way to resolving these issues in advance. This is, after all, what it means to become Real.

> *Being emotionally freed to admit life's fragility and our inevitable mortality helps us appreciate the life we enjoy right now. Facing rather than denying death helps us to celebrate life.*
>
> —David G. Myers,
> *The Pursuit of Happiness*

Retiring but Not Shy

As we've discussed in an earlier chapter, retirement isn't what it used to be. More women are working into their retirement years, and working in a whole new way after retiring, than ever before. The desire for a successful and productive retirement may be the goal that prompted you to read this book. If not, it's something you've been working on without fully realizing it. For the baby boom generation — 76 million of whom will turn sixty-five between 2011 and 2029 — retirement will have a different look and feel to it, and many of your peers will use this time to embark on the search that you have already begun.

But as a retiree, you can't just walk back into the labor market and expect open arms to catch you. You have to figure out what you want to do, how much time you want to spend at it, whether you want this new work to be primary or secondary to your everyday life, where those jobs are, and most important, what training you need.

A recently retired Marine colonel who had worked in human resources for three decades was considering offering his employment skills as an independent consultant . . . but his work was not his passion, never had been. After talking with other entrepreneurs at a networking meeting, he confessed that what he really loved to do was pilot boats around inland waterways. Within six months, he found a way to get paid for doing just that — by the U.S. Coast Guard.

Great retirements, like great careers, are no mistake. Their owners know a secret: they concluded somewhere along the line that the only security you can expect from your work life comes from within — not from the company, the university, or any other organization you work for. Career self-reliance is built on taking full responsibility. All jobs should be approached as if you are self-employed, regardless of who your boss may be. Instead of striving to climb the corporate ladder — often dropping core values on the way up — self-reliant workers care enough about their own development to acquire new skills and knowledge continually. The women and men who don't let life happen to them, but make life happen for them, use every job they hold as a springboard to the next phase of their maturing process. To these people, retirement is no exception in their lifelong quest for growth and fulfillment.

You can certainly consult someone familiar with your interests and your work who can provide honest feedback about your abilities. Professional career counseling can achieve the same thing. A nonprofit organization called Career Encores provides information and referral services to job seekers fifty and over. New Directions is an outplacement firm for senior executives in Boston; it frequently helps clients turn hobbies into paying enterprises.

Computer literacy is a necessity in today's employment marketplace. SeniorNet is a nonprofit organization whose goal is computer education for people fifty-five and older. For minimal fees, its seventy-five learning centers nationwide connect volunteers with seniors to teach the full range of computer skills.

One fallacy is that people get jobs by finding them in the classified advertisements. In 1994, small businesses created 80 percent of new jobs, and they relied mostly on referrals to acquire new employees. They never advertised at all! In today's workplace, networking is what results in jobs — and I'm not talking about your immediate circle of friends and family, although they should certainly know your aspirations. You can apply your Visioncrafting skills to network as if your life depended on it — because it does.

It may help to think of job seeking as your present job. If you need or want employment badly enough, spend eight hours a day pursuing contacts. The process of networking can be initiated by making a list of nearly everyone you know. Contact them all, making sure you customize your description of your job search for each one. Without fail, ask who else they think you might contact to pursue your ambition. This is how networks are expanded. You can also increase your confidence by meeting with other people who share similar circumstances. You might learn that you're not alone or that your talents are stronger than you imagined.

One of the great things about aging is that you get to be all the ages you've already been. That's a storehouse of learning, practice, knowledge, observation, exposure, and seasoning. You have more talent for living than you've ever had before. You even have the advantage of knowing which things you don't like. Doesn't it seem a waste to let what William Shakespeare called "the crown of life, our play's last act" be a deceleration, a limitation, a loss?

> *"How pleasant is the day when we give up striving to be young — or slender! Thank God! we say, those illusions are gone. Everything added to the Self is a burden as well as a pride."*
>
> —WILLIAM JAMES

THE FINAL MILES

We all have a need for community, to be part of a team, to make a contribution, to leave a legacy. You may never get to a carnival in Rio, dance on the great wall of China, or raft the rapids of the Grand Canyon, but you can make a list of the things you want to do. That is the accomplishment you bring away from your reading of this book. If you check it often and keep adding items, you'll be surprised how many you can make happen.

After you have pursued your goal for a while you may experience what marathon runners call "hitting the wall." This is the feeling, after about twenty of a marathon's 26.2 miles, that you simply can't go on, can't take another step. The famous Boston Marathon, which celebrated its 100th running in 1996, has a stretch of the course that has been aptly named Heartbreak Hill.

This is the point where you may feel you are running in place, getting nowhere on your own heartbreak hill. Progress seems to be beyond the limits of your endurance. The runners who finish races, even though they hit the wall, learn to dig deeper into their mental reserves — to ignore pain and exhaustion. They push themselves mentally with positive thoughts, which mobilizes them physically to complete the challenge. They imagine the feeling of exuberance as they cross the finish line, the roar of the crowd, their friends there to greet them, the tidal wave of achievement — even how good it will feel to stop and sit down.

This point in a race, when your body says no and your brain says yes, can be expected in any worthwhile effort. In the final miles you are alone. You have to believe in yourself. No one is going to magically appear on the sidelines to give you a ride or talk you through it.

But, as I've said before, this doesn't mean you have to go it alone; it simply means that finding supportive companions is up to you. It's okay to seek safety in numbers. For our ancestors, survival was based on herding together. If you belonged to a group, you could feel safe. For women, this has primarily meant having a relationship. Today, although that is still important, safety is secured in ways other than being attached to a man. A women now has more options and can anchor her dreams to whatever carries the most meaning for her. For you, it can be work, family, community, religion. Don't hesitate to use these touchstones as your source of strength and stability. A quest doesn't have to be lonely.

> *"Obstacles are those frightful things you see when you take your eyes off your goal."*
> —HENRY FORD

PAUSE FOR CELEBRATION

In today's roadrunner-speed world, rarely do we stop to mark an achievement. Can you think of something you did that deserved recognition but never was heralded — or even noticed — by others? Somewhere along the line, most of us were never told that we could celebrate more than federal holidays. If you look around, feats to celebrate are everywhere. In the current family of parents and 2.3 kids, there's bound to be some small victory every week.

As you pursue your goal, aided by your new team of friends and family, make it a habit to celebrate — even the smallest of victories. If you are starting a business, celebrate your first customer or contract. If you have a new job, celebrate completing the first week. If you absolutely must use your bonus money to pay bills, find some way to honor the fact that you were rewarded with a bonus: Go to a movie. Buy a new book. You deserve it.

BETTY

One of my clients, Betty, grew up in a house where pats on the back were few and far between. She never knew what it was like to have someone praise what she did. At major events like her high school graduation, her family dutifully attended, then went directly home afterwards and that was it. No party, no cake, no family or friends, no present.

When I was helping Betty, at every step of the way towards her goal we celebrated in my office verbally. I used the word "congratulations" when she was able to change the way she related to someone or when she completed a project at work.

Carrying this one step further, Betty informed her family that when she told them of a significant accomplishment, she expected them to find some way to acknowledge it. To her surprise and delight, after she received a promotion at work, her husband and kids took her out to her favorite restaurant. Betty had discovered and expressed a need to celebrate her triumphs — no matter how large or small — and her family responded.

I hope that by now you've decided to stop looking for the love of your life — that knight on a white horse to conduct your quest for you — and to find the life you love. I hope you wake up enthusiastic each day, thrilled to be doing what you have chosen — even if sometimes you feel anxious or scared. When you chase your dreams, every day feels like the gift it is, so you make it count 100 percent. Life is not a dress rehearsal — it's your one and only chance.

Sometime soon, when you are alone, give yourself a standing ovation. You have figured out how to write the script of your own life and give it the performance it deserves. Now I must confess that I have no exercise or meter to tell you when you have achieved your goal — because you don't need one. Success or happiness or nirvana or well-being — or whatever you want to call it — lies in your persistent, everyday progress toward the next green light. It's the pride of saying to yourself, "I did that." It's a wonderful feeling of accomplishment coupled with a keen sense of permanence.

When you succeed in going with the flow of your vision, you are likely to realize something else: what you wanted all along was what you needed all along. All these exercises and discussions have been nothing more than a road map to a destination that has always been within you — and easily within your reach: It's a place called your potential.

Dorothy and her friends traveled the yellow brick road in hopes of finding the Land of Oz, that magical place where they would find their inner power. The journey was fraught with danger but when they reached their destination, each realized that their inner strengths had been there all along. Learn from Dorothy: Look no farther than your own backyard; what you long for is already there, waiting to be actualized.

The Light That Never Fails

At first, re-visioning your life is like steering through a long, dark tunnel. You're unnerved without the accustomed light of routine; you see no alternatives at first so you keep going; you slow down, trying to adjust to the new conditions. Then, as you identify your dream, even though you're not sure where you'll end up, you emerge from the tunnel. Suddenly — perhaps for the first time in your life — you can see far ahead. You accelerate, losing your anxiety and gaining clarity of vision. You see choices, more and more roads to go down if you want. And best of all, there's plenty of room for everyone — all the people you love — to come along on the ride of your life.

The exercises you completed, which I hope you will refer to again from time to time, will never pinpoint exactly where you ought to go or who you ought to be. Rather, they help you chart where you want to go, once you know who you are. To keep creating the life you want, you don't need the next self-help bestseller, a weekend retreat, or witchcraft; you need to return to the techniques you've learned here when things stop feeling right. When you feel lost, pull over and consult the map.

You've read about other women who altered their course at different intersections — even when their destination was in sight. All the roads are right, and none are too long when you are on the avenue of your destiny.

FOR THOSE WHO FOLLOW YOU

As you read this book, it's quite likely that you had to distinguish between what your parents wanted and expected from you, and what *you* wanted and expected in life. If you have managed to separate these two compelling forces, you have performed a labor of love — for yourself and them. You managed to shed their images and sketch a new you.

Some of my clients ask what they can do in raising their sons and daughters, to make the process described in this book come more naturally to the next generation. I'm always encouraged by this question, because it shows how much they value the transition and their commitment to passing on the cycle of success to the next generation.

To look that far forward, we need to look back. Women have traditionally used helplessness to get what they want. Only in the last seventy-five years has the need to overcome their powerlessness been publicly expressed. Women have traditionally feared success and its accompanying power because their sense of self is tied to their need for attachment and connection.

To answer our original question about your daughters, women need internal as well as external applause. A common denominator for successful women is having received a positive message from their mothers. By positive message, I mean it is critical for daughters to see their mothers as equal partners to their fathers — and as commanding respect in all their relationships. It is not healthy for a daughter to watch her mother accept treatment as a second-class citizen who can't control her own direction. When a mother is a self-reliant, self-competent individual, then the daughter can identify with her and develop her own separate and competent Self.

So you see, as you proceed toward your goal, that an invaluable by-product, requiring no extra effort, is the influence your quest has on your children. While you are exploring *your* wants and needs, give your daughters and sons permission to do it too.

Another means of encouraging daughters to pursue their dreams as adults comes from developmental studies. According to psychologist Dr. Daniel Levinson of Yale University, the author of *The Seasons of a Man's Life,* men have a developmental life stage he calls "the dream." In this phase, between the ages of seventeen and twenty-eight, they experience early adulthood. This involves a vague sense of self, somewhere between a fantasy of the future and a well-conceived plan.

Many females don't have this. They usually live in sequential phases — without these premonitions and rehearsals — unless they are prompted. Once in a while, for fun, sit down with your daughters and ask them what they like doing, where they see themselves five years from now, ten years from now.

What about sons? Gloria Steinem encourages us to continue to examine gender roles. She points out that we have acquired the courage to raise our daughters more like our sons, but few parents have ventured to raise their sons to be more like their daughters. If we instill in our children the sense that all tasks — from dishwashing to snow shoveling — are gender-free, it will go a long way toward paving the road for women of the next generation when their time comes to chase a dream.

By the same token, Steinem points out that although women have convinced themselves they can do what men can do, women have not yet convinced themselves — and therefore those around them — that men can do what women can do. You may be striving to manage your life so that you can pursue your goal by recruiting the help of other women (a cleaning person, an administrative assistant, a child care provider) when many of the tasks you are delegating to women could be done by your partner or your son.

For those times when you worry about restarting your engine and steering onto the road, and you wonder why you began this journey in the first place, I leave you with my last list. Write this down, post it on the refrigerator, or carry it around with you for a while — as I hope you'll carry all your new discoveries in your heart and mind. *Bon voyage!*

Fifteen Resolutions for Turning Red Lights to Green Lights
1. DREAM TILL YOU DROP.
2. FORMULATE YOUR MISSION; WRITE A CONTRACT WITH YOURSELF.
3. BE OR BECOME OPTIMISTIC.
4. NEVER USE THE FOUR-LETTER WORD "CAN'T."
5. CONSIGN REGRETS TO THE PAST; THAT WAS THEN, THIS IS NOW.
6. DON'T BLAME OTHERS FOR YOUR PAST MISTAKES.
7. PLAN, PLAN, PLAN.
8. TAKE CALCULATED, REALISTIC RISKS; TAKE BABY STEPS.
9. DO IT SCARED, IF NECESSARY.
10. EXPECT DETOURS; BE FLEXIBLE.
11. REVISE IF NECESSARY.
12. ALWAYS HAVE A BACKUP PLAN.
13. RECRUIT OTHERS TO HELP YOU.
14. DON'T LET OTHERS DERAIL YOU.
15. BELIEVE YOU DESERVE FULFILLMENT AND EXUBERANCE; BECOME YOUR OWN CHEERLEADER.

*R*esources

CHOOSING A CAREER

John Caple, *Finding the Hat That Fits: How to Turn Your Heart's Desire into Your Life's Work.* New York: Dutton, 1993.

Marti Chaney and Vicki Thayer, *Childhood Dreams — Career Answers: A Woman's Practical and Playful Guide to the Career Puzzle.* Salem, Oregon: Lifeworks Press, 1992.

Edgar H. Schein, *Career Anchors: Discovering Your Real Values.* San Diego, California: Pfeiffer, 1993.

Barbara Sher and Barbara Smith, *I Could Do Anything If I Only Knew What It Was: How to Discover What You Really Want and How to Get It.* New York: Delacorte, 1994.

Paul D. Tieger and Barbara Barron-Tieger, *Do What You Are: Discover the Perfect Career for You Through the Secrets of Personality Type.* Boston: Little, Brown, 1992.

Motivation Research Group, *Kuder Career Search Schedule,* Atlanta. This IBM-compatible computer diskette matches people to jobs they are likely to enjoy.

NCS Career Magazine. Internet address: http:// www.careermag.com/ index.shtml/. This on-line magazine contains articles to help begin and continue a career search. Includes a job search database and a career-discussion forum.

GETTING ORGANIZED

All-In-One Business Planning Guide. Holbrook, Mass.: Adams Media Corporation, 1994. Offers advice on how to create plans for marketing, sales, and finance.

Jeffrey Mayer, *Time Management for Dummies.* Braintree, Mass.: IDG Books, 1995.

Covey Leadership Center, Provo, Utah. Internet address: http://www.covey.com/, or call (888) 652-6839. Offers planning materials by mail, including the First Things First Time-Management course ($195 per person), or the 7 Habits Organizer Kit ($65).

Day Runner: Fullerton, California. Internet address http://www.dayrunner.com/, or call (800) 635-5544. Sells a classic $5^1/_2$-inch by $8^1/_2$-inch planner ($55), as well as the electronic Day Runner Planner for Windows ($75).

Day-Timer: Allentown, Pennsylvania. (800) 225-5005. Offers cassettes and videos on how to get organized.

Filofax: Norwalk, Connecticut. (800) 783-9590. Sells the Epping Organizer ($160).

Franklin Quest: Salt Lake City; (800) 914-1776. Sells day planners and binders, and also offers the TimeQuest seminar.

NETWORKING

Cynthia Chin-Lee, *It's Who You Know: Career Strategies for Making Effective Personal Contacts.* San Diego, California: Pfeiffer, 1993.

James Gray, *Winning Image: Present Yourself with Confidence and Style for Career Success.* New York: AMACOM, 1993.

Douglas B. Richardson, *Networking.* New York: Wiley, 1994.

RESUMES

Robert F. Wilson and Erik H. Rambusch, *Conquer Resume Objections.* New York: Wiley, 1994.

Resumail Network. Internet address: http:// www.resumail.com/. Helps site visitors build smarter resumes. Currently the software is free.

The Adams Resume Almanac. Adams Media Corporation, 1994. Contains six hundred resume examples and fifty attention-getting cover letters. Covers positions from entry-level to senior executive.

JOB SEEKING

Caroline Bird, *Second Careers: New Ways to Work after Fifty.* Boston: Little, Brown, 1992.

Ralph W. Cameron, *The Minority Executives Handbook: The Complete Guide to Career Success in Today's Culturally Diverse Workforce.* Washington, D.C.: Amistad, 1989. Provides tips and advice on getting promoted and protecting against discrimination in the workplace.

William Charland, *Career-Shifting: Starting Over in a Changing Economy.* Holbrook, Mass.: Adams Media Corporation, 1993.

Gerry Crispin and Mark Mehler, *Career X Roads.* MMC Group, 1997. Directory of job, resume, and career management sites on the World Wide Web. Free updates–register via e-mail: mmc@careerxroads.com/.

John A. Hornaday and Lucinda A. Gibson, *The Kuder Book of People Who Like Their Work.* Atlanta: Motivation Research Group. A collection of 1,460 job descriptions provided by people who hold the jobs and enjoy their work. Describes the personality traits and abilities needed for job success, job duties, a typical day, and educational prerequisites for each job. Also available on disk.

Les Krantz, *The World Almanac Job Finders Guide 1997.* Mahwah, New Jersey: World Almanac Books, 1996. Contains advice on how to network the hidden job market and negotiate the right salary.

Dan Moreau, *Kiplinger's Survive and Profit from a Mid-Career Change.* New York: Kiplinger Books, 1994.

Stephen M. Pollan and Mark Levine, *Starting Over: How to Change Careers or Start Your Own Business.* New York: Warner, 1997. Weighs the risks and rewards of career change. Contains an excellent resource section.

Margaret F. Riley, *The Guide to Internet Job Searching.* Lincolnwood, Illinois: VGM Career Books, 1996.

Nancy K. Schlossberg and Susan Porter Robinson, *Going to Plan B.* New York: Fireside, 1996.

Joyce Schwarz, *Successful ReCareering.* Franklin Lakes, New Jersey: Career Press, 1993.

Adams JobBank Online. Internet address: http://www.adamsonline.com/. Adams Media Corporation provides leads to technical, management, computer, and medical jobs. Also includes a career center that includes company profiles, strategies, and job-fair listings.

America's Job Bank. Internet address: http://www.ajb.dni.us. Contains information on approximately 250,000 jobs, from professional and technical to blue collar. Includes listings from 1,800 state employment service offices throughout the United States.

Boldface Jobs. Internet address: http://www.boldface.com/. Recruiters post national positions on this site. Currently, you can post your resume free for thirty days.

Careers and Jobs. Internet address: http://www.starthere.com/jobs/. Provides hundreds of job listings and links to other job-seekers.

Career Resource Center. Internet address: http://www.careers.org/. Contains thousands of national and international job openings, listed both alphabetically and geographically.

CareerMosaic. Internet address: http://www.careermosaic.com/. Contains thousands of job listings in all occupations worldwide. Provides helpful job-hunting tips, employer profiles and direct links to corporations currently hiring.

CareerPath. Internet address: http://www.careerpath.com. Resources for job seekers looking for positions in or near major US cities. Includes Sunday job listings from the *New York Times,* the *Washington Post,* the *Chicago Tribune,* the *Los Angeles Times,* and the *Boston Globe,* plus other major metropolitan newspapers.

Dejanews. Internet address: http://www.dejanews.com/. Information on finding the best chat rooms for your job search.

E-Span. Internet address: http://www.espan.com/. Approximately ten thousand job listings are updated daily.

Federal Jobs. Internet address: http://www.fedworld.gov/jobs/. Posts nationwide government jobs.

Internet Business Network. Internet address: http://www.interbiznet. com/eeri/. Links job recruiting sites for hundreds of industries, ranging from engineering to sports.

MedSearch America. Internet address: http:/www.medsearch.com/. Contains listings of some 1,900 health-care jobs.

NationJob Network. Internet address: http://www.nationjob.com/. Offers job listings gathered from newspapers, businesses, and other sources. The site's personal job scout, P.J. Scout, searches for jobs based upon your preferences, qualifications, and background and returns leads via e-mail.

Monster Board. Internet address: http://www.monster.com/. Contains approximately 20,000 job listings, updated daily.

National Business Employment Weekly. Internet address: http://www. nbew.com/. Dow Jones News Service. Lists hundreds of national and regional employment opportunities and advice on how to land them.

Online Career Center. Internet address: http:// www.occ.com/. Approximately 55,000 job listings, updated daily.

The Women's Wire. Internet address: http:// www.women.com/.

CAREER STRATEGY GROUPS
Exec-U-Net. (800) 637-3126. A career networking company based in Norwalk, Conn. Allows you to hook up with career counselors.

Five O'Clock Club. (800) 538-6645 ext. 600. A career strategy group based in New York.

CAREER COACHING
Coach University. Internet address: http://www.coachu.com/, or call (800) 482-6224. Helps individuals set goals and gives people the push they need to get started and stay on course.

International Coach Federation. Internet address: http://www. coachfederation.org/, or call (888) 423-3131. Free referral service.

EDUCATION

CERTIFICATE AND DEGREE PROGRAMS

Richard Koonce, *Career Power.* New York: AMACOM, 1994. Lists certificate programs available in many fields.

Catapult: Summer Work, Internships, Fieldwork, and Postgraduate Options. Internet address: http://www.jobeb.org/Catapult/jintern. html/. One-stop shopping for people looking for work opportunities with companies, schools, and nonprofit organizations.

Distance Learning Office. Internet address: http://unix.dce.ksu.edu/ dce/c8distan.html/.

Distance Learning Options. Internet address: http://www.isc. rit.edu/~6.

EDTECH Archive: Finding Distance Learning Programs. Internet address: http://h-net.msu.edu/~edw/.

Virtual University — Western Governors University. Internet address: http://www.eecs.wsu.edu/. Virtual two- and four-year programs spanning twelve Western states. Log on to the homepage and download class material. Good for parents with full-time jobs.

STARTING YOUR OWN BUSINESS

GETTING LAUNCHED

Claudia Jessup and Genie Chipps, *The Woman's Guide to Starting a Business.* New York: Henry Holt, 1991. Advice on how to turn your ideas into a profit-making venture.

Eric Siegel and Brian R. Ford, *The Ernst & Young Business Plan Guide.* New York: Wiley, 1993.

NFIB Online. Internet address: http://www.nfibonline.com/. Launched by the 600,000-member National Federation of Independent Businesses. Offers daily features for small business owners.

Service Corps of Retired Executives (202) 205-6762. Active and retired businesspeople offering free assistance to help set up a business.

Barbara Littman, *The Woman's Business Resource Guide.* Chicago: Contemporary Books, 1996.

Yahoo!'s Small Business Information. Internet address: http://www.
yahoo.com/. Directory of more than one hundred small-business-
related websites including American Express's Small Business
Exchange (Internet address: http://www.americanexpress.com/
smallbusiness/), Entrepreneurs on the Web (http://www.
eotw.com/), and Microsoft's Smallbiz (http://www.microsoft.
com/smallbiz/).

WORKING AT HOME

Mike Antoniak, *How to Start a Home-Based Business.* New York:
Avon, 1995.

Bernard J. David, *Entrepreneurial PC: The Complete Guide to Starting
a PC-Based Business.* New York: McGraw-Hill, 1994.

Paul and Sarah Edwards, *The Best Home Businesses for the 90's.* New
York: Tarcher/Putnam, 1995.

David R. Eyler, *Home Business Desk Reference: Everything You Need to
Know to Start and Run Your Home-Based Business.* New York:
Wiley, 1994.

Kim T. Gordon, *Growing Your Home-Based Business: A Complete Guide to
Proven Sales and Marketing Communication Strategies.* Englewood,
New Jersey: Prentice-Hall, 1992.

Daryl A. Hall, *One Thousand One Hundred One Businesses You Can
Start from Home.* New York: Wiley, 1995.

Daniel S. Janal, *101 Businesses You Can Start on the Internet.* New York:
Van Nostrand Reinhold, 1996.

Edna Sheedy, *Start and Run a Profitable Home-Based Business: Your Step-
by-Step First Year Guide.* Bellingham, Washington: Self-Counsel
Press, 1994.

Julian L. Simon, *How to Start and Operate a Mail-Order Business.* New
York: McGraw-Hill, 1993.

WHERE TO GET FINANCING

EDUCATION

Daniel Cassidy, *Worldwide Graduate Scholarship Directory.* Franklin Lakes, New Jersey: Career Press, 1996. (800) 227-3371.

Anna Leider, *Loans and Grants from Uncle Sam: Am I Eligible and for How Much?* Chicago: Dearborn, 1995.

Paul Phifer, *College Majors & Careers: A Resource Guide for Effective Life Planning.* Deerfield, Florida: Garrett, 1993.

Joseph M. Re, *Earn and Learn: Your Guide to In-School Educational Employment Programs.* Chicago: Dearborn, 1995.

Debra L. Wexler, *College Checkmate: Innovative Tuition Plans That Make You a Winner.* Chicago: Dearborn, 1995.

The Back-to-School Money Book: A Financial Aid Guide for Midlife and Older Women Seeking Education and Training, 1996-1998. AARP Publications, 601 E St. NW Washington, DC 20049 (http://www.aarp.org). Free booklet lists sources of financial aid and provides creative ways to help reduce educational expenses.

College Board. Internet address: http://www.collegeboard.org/.

CollegeNet. Internet address: http://www.collegenet.com/.

FastWeb. Internet address: http://www.fastweb.com/.

FinAid. Internet address: http://www.finaid.org/.

SRN Express. Internet address: http://www.rams.com/srn/.

Xap Corp. Internet address: http://www.xap.com/.

The Education Resource Institute. 330 Stuart Street, Boston, Mass. 02116. (800) 255-8372.

National Health Service Corps. Scholarship Program, 207 Chain Bridge Road, Vienna, VA 22182. (800) 221-9393.

Stafford Loan Program. The Federal Student Aid Information Center, P.O. Box 84, Washington, D.C. 20044. (800) 433-3243.

BUSINESS

Bruce Blechman and Jay Conrad Levinson, *Guerrilla Financing: Alternative Techniques to Finance Any Small Business.* Boston: Houghton Mifflin, 1991.

Max Fallek, *Finding Money for Your Small Business: The One-Stop Guide to Raising All the Money You Will Need.* Chicago: Dearborn Financial, 1994.

Bryan E. Milling, *How To Get A Loan or Line of Credit.* Naperville, Illinois: Source Books, 1997. Covers what type of loan you need, how to negotiate, SBA vs. other loans; includes step-by-step financial forms.

Women Inc. A nonprofit concern in Sacramento, California. Has agreements with major commercial banks to get its 30,000 members access to loans. Special loan officers give prospective borrowers assistance in getting approved.

RETIREMENT

Delos Marsh, *Retirement Careers: Combining The Best of Work and Leisure.* Charlotte, Vermont: Williams Publishers., 1991. Offers advice on consulting and other retirement work and volunteering opportunities.

Kathryn and Ross Petras, *The Only Retirement Guide You'll Ever Need.* New York: Fireside, 1991.

Lisa A. Rogak and David H. Bangs, Jr., *100 Best Retirement Businesses.* Chicago: Upstart Publishing Co., Inc., 1994. Good for preretirement planning or career change. Includes several interviews with business owners on the pros and cons of their choice of business.

David Savageau, *Retirement Places Rated.* New York: Macmillan, 1995. One hundred and eighty top retirement areas are ranked and compared.

Finding the Right Place for Retirement. $4 plus 75¢ shipping and handling from 50 Plus Pre-Retirement Services, 28 West 23rd Street, New York, NY 10010.

How to Plan and Execute a Successful Retirement Relocation. $3.95 plus $2.25 shipping and handling from Where to Retire, Augusta Drive, suite 415, Houston, TX 77057.

Homebuyer's Fair. Internet address: http://www.homefair.com. Helps determine living costs in potential retirement locations.

ReloSmart. $79.99 for Windows or Mac version; (800) 872-2294. Helps you figure the cost of living and taxes in potential relocation sites.

ORGANIZATIONS OF INTEREST

American Association for Consumer Benefits, P.O. Box 100279, Fort Worth, TX 76185. (800) 872-8896.

American Home Business Association. Internet address: http://www. homebusiness.com/, or call (800) 664-2422. A 35,000-member group offering discounted phone service, group health insurance, and help in setting up retirement IRAs.

American Small Business Association, 1800 N. Kent Street, Arlington, VA 22209. (800) 235-3298.

American Woman's Economic Development Corporation, 71 Vanderbilt Avenue, New York, NY 10169, (212) 692-9100.

Consumer Federation of America, 1424 16th Street N.W., Washington, D.C. 20036. (202) 387-0087). Will analyze all life insurance policies.

Health Insurance Association of America. Internet address: http:// www.insure.com, or call (888) 844-2782. Offers help on buying life, home, and auto insurance.

Home Executives National Networking Association, P.O. Box 6223, Bloomingdale, IL 60108. (708) 307-7130.

Mothers' Home Business Network, P.O. Box 423, East Meadow, NY 11554. (516) 997-7394.

National Association of Home-Based Businesses, P.O. Box 30220, Baltimore, MD 21270. (410) 363-3698.

National Association for the Self-Employed. Internet address: http://www.nase.org/, or call (800) 232-NASE. This is the largest organization in the United States of businesses with four or fewer employees (yearly membership fee $72). Offers low-cost health insurance and a toll-free hotline that answers business questions.

Service Corps of Retired Executives Association, 409 3rd Street S.W., Washington, D.C. 20024. (202) 205-6762.

Small Business Administration. Internet address: http://www.sbaonline. sba.gov/.

Small Business Assistance Center, 554 Main Street, P.O. Box 1441, Worcester, MA 01601. (508) 756-3513. Offers planning and strategy programs to help start, improve, or expand a business.

Support Services Alliance, (800) 322-3920. A 10,000 member association for the self-employed. Offers discounts on life and dental insurance, and as much as 40 percent off tax preparation.

RECONNECTING WITH NATURE

Michael J. Cohen, Ed.D. Ecopress, *Reconnecting with Nature: FindingWellness through Restoring your Bond with the Earth.* 1997. Internet address: http://www.pacificrim.net/~ nature/, or e-mail at info@ igc.org.

VOLUNTEERING

American Hiking Society — Volunteer Vacations, Box 20160, Washington, D.C. 20041. (301) 565-6704. Help restore America's 300,000-mile trail system.

America's Promise. Internet address: http://www.americaspromise.org/.

Corporation For National Service. Internet address: http://www.cns.gov/. A listing of government-sponsored opportunities.

IdeaList. Internet address: http://www.contact.org/.

Bill McMillon, *Volunteer Vacations.* Chicago: Chicago Review Press, 1997.

Earthwatch of Boston. Internet address: http://www.earthwatch.com/, or call them at (800) 776-0188.

Global Service Corps. Internet address: http://www.econet.apc.org/ei/ gsc/gschome.html, or call them at (415) 788-3666.

Global Volunteers. Internet address: http://www.globalvlntrs.org/ home.htm, or call them at (800) 487-1074.

The Nature Conservancy, 1815 N. Lynn St., Arlington, VA 22029.(800) 628-6860. Help maintain 8.3 million acres of endangered natural habitats in the U.S.

National Park Service, Interior Building, Box 37127, Washington, D.C. 20013. (202) 523-0582. Internet address: http://www.nps.gov/ volunteer/.

National Audubon Society, 700 Broadway, New York, New York 10003. (212) 979-3000. Help restore ecosystems that support wildlife.

BIBLIOGRAPHY

Claudia Bepko and Jo-Ann Krestan. *Too Good for Her Own Good.* New York: HarperCollins, 1990.

LeslieBeth Berger. *Women, Work & Incest.* Springfield, IL: Charles C. Thomas, 1998.

Les Brown. *Live Your Dreams.* New York: Avon Books, 1992.

David D. Burns. *Feeling Good: The New Mood Therapy.* New York: Signet, 1980.

Mihaly Csikszentmihalyi. *Flow: The Psychology of Optimal Experience.* New York: Harper & Row, 1990.

Clarissa Pinkola Estes. *Women Who Run with the Wolves.* New York: Ballantine, 1992.

Roger Fisher and Scott Brown. *Getting Together.* New York: Penguin Books, 1988.

Betty Friedan. *The Fountain of Age.* New York: Simon & Schuster, 1989.

Carol Gilligan. *In a Different Voice.* Cambridge, MA: Harvard University Press, 1982.

Napoleon Hill. *Think & Grow Rich.* New York: Ballantine Books, 1960.

Susan Jeffers. *Feel the Fear and Do It Anyway.* New York: Fawcett Columbine, 1987.

Ruthellen Josselson. *Finding Herself.* San Francisco: Jossey-Bass, 1987.

Carol Klein and Richard Gotti. *Overcoming Regret.* New York: Bantam Books, 1992.

Harold Kushner. *When All You've Ever Wanted Isn't Enough.* New York: Simon & Schuster, 1986.

Harriet Goldhor Lerner. *The Dance of Anger.* New York: Harper & Row, 1985.

Daniel J. Levinson. *The Seasons of a Man's Life.* New York: Ballantine, 1978.

Barbara Mackoff. *Growing a Girl.* Dell Publishing Group, Inc., 1996.

Jean Baker Miller. *Toward a New Psychology of Women.* Boston: Beacon Press, 1976.

Joy Miller. *My Holding You Up Is Holding Me Back.* Deerfield Beach, FL: Health Communications, Inc., 1991.

David G. Myers. *The Pursuit of Happiness.* New York: Avon Books, 1992.

Norman Vincent Peale. *You Can If You Think You Can.* New York: Fawcett Crest Books, 1974.

Rick Pitino. *Success Is a Choice: Ten Steps to Overachieving in Business and Life.* New York: Broadway Books, 1997.

Anthony Robbins. *Awaken the Giant Within.* New York: Penguin Books, 1988.

Nancy K. Schlossberg and Susan Porter Robinson. *Going to Plan B.* New York: Simon & Schuster, 1996.

Martin E.P. Seligman. *Learned Optimism.* New York: Alfred A. Knopf, 1991.

Gail Sheehy. *New Passages.* New York: Random House, 1995.

Barbara Sher with Annie Gottlieb. *Wishcraft.* New York: Ballantine Books, 1979.

Sidney B. Simon. *Getting Unstuck.* New York: Warner, 1988.

Gloria Steinem. *Revolution from Within: A Book of Self-Esteem.* New York: Vanity Fair, 1992.

Deborah Tannen, *You Just Don't Understand.* New York: Morrow, 1990.

Index

AARP. *See* American Association of Retired Persons
abandonment, fear of, 10, 21
abilities, using existing, 148. *See also* skills
academics, internal locus of control and, 45
accomplishments, listing, 89
achievements
    finding alternate routes to goals, 113–114
    happiness and, 45
    internal growth as, 99
    listing, 89–94
    reminding yourself of past, 138
    success and practicing new habits, 148
achievers, nurturers becoming, 125–126, 145–148
adulthood. *See* second adulthood
advice, consulting with friends, 82
aging
    activity and, 72
    education and, 72–73
    fear of, 21
    mid-life crisis and, 70–71
    rating responses about, 14
    retirement and, 72–73, 189–191, 207
    second adulthood and, 71
    transitional generation, *xx*
    workforce and, 72
all-or-nothing thinking, negative self-chatter and, 31
ambitions, defining, 82
American Association of Retired Persons, 73
analytical skills, identifying, 90–91
anger
    acknowledging, 180

as a learned response, 53
    letting family members express, 178–179
    recognizing your, 180–181
anxiety
    derailing the worry cycle, 138–140
    helplessness and, 54
    learning to manage, 7
    marriage and, 29
    as a warning signal, 135–138
apologizing, 167–172
approval, seeking, 36, 155
arguments, using to challenge negative thinking, 60
Ash, Mary Kay, 122
aspirations
    education and, 6, 30
    emotions and, 97
    dismissing with negative self-chatter, 29
    family members blocking, 145–147
    focusing on, 78–79
    listing creative, 20–21
    setting too low, 121
    survey results of women's, *xx*
    See also goals
assumptions, testing, 124–126

behavior
    beliefs and, 31
    passive-aggressive, 174–176
beliefs
    behavior and, 31
    internal and external, 57–58
    irrational, 26–27
    overgeneralization of, 31